Tools for Energized Teaching

Tools for Energized Teaching

Revitalize Instruction with Ease

Kenneth L. Wilson

Teacher Ideas Press, an imprint of Libraries Unlimited
Westport, Connecticut • London

Library of Congress Cataloging-in-Publication Data

Wilson, Kenneth L.
　Tools for energized teaching : revitalize instruction with ease / by Kenneth L. Wilson.
　　　p. cm
　Includes bibliographical references and index.
　ISBN 0-325-00770-5 (pbk. : alk. paper)
　1. Teaching 2. Education—Research. I. Title.
LB1025.3W53　2006
371.102—dc22　　　2006007602

British Library Cataloguing in Publication Data is available.

Copyright © 2006 by Kenneth L. Wilson

All rights reserved. No part of this book may be
reproduced in any form or by any electronic or mechanical means,
including information storage and retrieval systems, without
permission in writing from the publisher, except by a reviewer, who
may quote brief passages in a review. An exception is made for
individual librarians and educators who may make copies of portions
of the scripts for classroom use. Reproducible pages may be copied
for classroom and educational programs only. Performances may be
videotaped for school or library purposes.

Library of Congress Catalog Card Number: 2006007602
ISBN: 0-325-00770-5

First published in 2006

Libraries Unlimited/Teacher Ideas Press, 88 Post Road West, Westport, CT 06881
A Member of the Greenwood Publishing Group, Inc.
www.lu.com

Printed in the United States of America

The paper used in this book complies with the
Permanent Paper Standard issued by the National
Information Standards Organization (Z39.48–1984).

10　9　8　7　6　5　4　3　2　1

Contents

Acknowledgments   vii
Introduction   ix

■ Section 1   Your Repertoire

Chapter 1	Easier, More Enjoyable Teaching	3

■ Section 2   The Tools

Chapter 2	The Power of Relationship	11
Chapter 3	Visual and Personalized Learning	16
Chapter 4	Learner-Centered Dialogue	26
Chapter 5	The Power of the Authentic	35
Chapter 6	The Enjoyment of Thinking	40
Chapter 7	The Joy of Language and Communication	53
Chapter 8	An Appreciation for Quality	65
Chapter 9	Collaboration and Celebration	70
Chapter 10	Your Playful Repertoire	77
Chapter 11	Simple, Familiar, and Versatile Tools	90
Chapter 12	Art, Drama, Music, and the Senses	108
Chapter 13	Learning for Life	115

■ Section 3   Your Repertoire, Your Wisdom, and Your Orchestration

Chapter 14	Your Repertoire in Action	131

Chapter 15	Upward Spirals	134
Chapter 16	Three Mental Maps	137
Chapter 17	Playing Around . . . Seriously	139
Chapter 18	Your Underachievers	141
Chapter 19	Being Inspired and Inspiring	147
Chapter 20	Advanced Orchestration	149

Bibliography 155
Index 157

Acknowledgments

This book began more than 20 years ago as a course book for my popular workshop "Energizing Your Classroom." Year after year I would borrow, steal, assimilate, synthesize, invent, and condense what I felt were enjoyable and effective ways to make teaching easier. A great number of people have contributed ideas that have made their way into this book. If you see anything here that was "your idea," I thank you and apologize if I have not given you credit.

Thank you, especially, to several people who have particularly inspired me or supported my work. First thanks go to my wife, Mary Wilson, who encouraged me, tolerated me, and made sure I didn't forget to eat while I was writing. Second, a very big thank you to my friend, colleague, educator/author, and Boci competitor, Ardie Cole. Ardie convinced me to get this work finished and published. Thanks to Mike and Maggie Seymour at the Heritage Institute, who are two exceedingly thoughtful, caring educators and humanitarians—and I have been fortunate to work with them for 10 years. And to my teacher friend Brad Linsday, I thank you for your enthusiastic experimentation with these tools, and the integrity you bring with you to education.

Many education researchers, authors, and presenters have influenced my own perspectives. Among these are Ted Sizer, Jim Fay, Robert Marzano, Grant Wiggins, William Glasser, Stephen Covey, Howard Gardner, Bob Garmston, Harry Wong, Edward de Bono, Eric Jensen, Madeline Hunter, Rachael Kessler, and others.

Introduction

■ Why This Book?

Teaching is nearly always demanding, and sometimes overwhelming. For that reason, one of the greatest needs that teachers have is for a larger repertoire of the most powerful and versatile techniques to make teaching easier and more enjoyable—and to do this as simply as possible *without* sacrificing excellence.

Few practical syntheses of this type exist—there are books of strategies for each of the content areas, for thinking skills, for self-esteem, for multiple intelligences, and so on. This book is a resource that has assimilated many of the most versatile and generic tools across each of these somewhat arbitrary disciplines. The result is a richness of tools made far more accessible and user-friendly.

No matter how you teach, what you teach, who you teach, or how long you have taught, this book's goal is to propel you further in the direction *you* want to go. Every effort has been made to incorporate and interconnect current education research and methods in ways that are jargon-free, and that lead to ready comprehension and practical application.

These ideas reflect my experience with thousands of teachers, in combination with such concepts and theories as systems thinking, peak performance, constructivist and brain-based learning, Covey's *Seven Habits* (2004), and psychotherapy. Plus decades of my own lifetime of successes and mistakes—though the mistakes taught me far more. (Mistakes always do.)

You won't find quick fixes here. No foolproof formulas. You'll still have to apply these techniques to your objectives, your students, your curriculum, and your teaching style.

■ Where to Begin

Where you begin depends on where you are, and where you want to go. Here are some suggestions.

New Teachers . . .

This is your starter tool kit. Get ready for some excitement—a synthesis of tools, strategies, and insights to truly energize any classroom. May you have many a runner's high from experimenting with these.

What to do now: Skim each section, highlighting those tools and ideas that excite you. Pick a small number to incorporate into your lessons this week, before you get too busy and forget them. Experiment—trial-and-error learning produces powerful results! But be sure not to go into overdrive; your students do need consistency and structure far more than they need novelty and change.

Experienced Educators . . .

This book is your creative reminder. Many of these ideas and strategies will be familiar to you in one form or another—you just need a little reminding to rekindle your excitement for so many things you have successfully done in past years.

What to do now: You may not want to be told "what to do now"—you have the experience to best identify fruitful and energizing opportunities for change. Merely keep an open mind—there are numerous surprises in here that can make your teaching easier, more enjoyable, and more successful.

Curriculum and Staff Development Leaders . . .

Here are a splendid variety of powerful, open-ended strategies borrowed from many disciplines within and beyond education. Each can be adapted, extended, combined, and otherwise changed in countless ways. You are the master chef—you are invited (urged!) to cook up your own exciting recipes. And be sure to at least skim the insights in Section Three.

What to do now: Tie these tools in with what you already know. The immediate benefit will be a richer, more varied curriculum or workshop.

Most significantly, though, these pages will prompt you to reflect, to synthesize, to construct new connections—to critically assess that which you took for granted, and to reaffirm that you which knew. Challenge yourself to break out of your old routines. Think anew.

Section 1
Your Repertoire

Teaching requires that you influence others. Put another way, teaching requires that you have the power to inspire students. This power stems in part from your orchestration of a rich repertoire that energizes both you and your students.

This notion of the importance of repertoire is not at all new. Pick up any book on education methods—classroom management, cooperative learning, thinking skills, instructional techniques, assessment, or multiple intelligences, for example. Implicit within any of these are the following:

> **1.** The essential requirement that the teacher have command of a variety of techniques.
> **2.** That these techniques be internalized and automatic enough that the teacher can simultaneously be engaged with the diverse multitasking demands of teaching.

Robert Marzano (2003), in summarizing research on classroom management techniques, came to the conclusion that "mental set" was the single most influential element in classroom management. Mental set, or "mindfulness" or "with-it-ness," is the state of heightened awareness and conscious control that good teachers display. *Yet, this ideal state is only possible when you can be running your repertoire (i.e., your tools) in your autopilot mode.* It is absolutely impossible to teach well consistently if you do not have an autopilot repertoire of techniques for managing and teaching your students. Your goal is to become increasingly automatic in your mastery of the tools. This frees up your consciousness and awareness to lead the orchestration of the whole.

Chapter 1
Easier, More Enjoyable Teaching

Where do you start with this repertoire? Your priority is to choose those relatively simple tools that will make the biggest difference for the least effort. And you want enjoyment—for yourself and your students. Sure, enjoyment can be elusive, yet few other pursuits are as pivotal to one's effectiveness in work and in life. For without enjoyment, most of one's efforts eventually lose vigor.

■ Applying Your Familiar Tools

As you practice using any tool, your efforts will become increasingly efficient. Furthermore, the tools will mold themselves to your personality, teaching style, and objectives. This is a very pleasant experience. You will "own" a repertoire that is uniquely you. Your teaching will evolve to be a more spontaneous, authentic, and joyful expression of who you are. To make your teaching a celebration of yourself *and* to be more effective at the same time—this is the pinnacle of teaching!

But first, realize that you already have a repertoire! Prior to enlarging your repertoire, you want to get the maximum mileage from the tools you already know. Seek especially those tools that create a high-trust, low-stress environment, where students are learning things that interest and challenge them.

As already implied, part of the mental high of teaching—the flow state—results from your own sense of ownership, your creativity, the positive emotion you exude when you are authentically engaged and alive, rather than following prepared curriculum materials. And not only that, it can be time-consuming to skim through your "dust-buddies" (i.e., your education materials that sit on the shelves for years collecting dust with their buddies) for next week's lesson, or tomorrow's worksheet. And even if you closely follow a commercial curriculum, you will always want the potential to instantly draw upon your own talent and wisdom to supplement even the best of these.

Remember, too, that kids respond to teachers who are authentically engaged with their teaching. This is not the same as "winging it." Rather, it is *fluid organization*—being organized and flexible at the same time. As a colleague of mine said, "You owe it to your students to teach this way."

This is powerful stuff! It isn't rocket science. But it is exceedingly satisfying. Here are a couple of examples to illustrate the power of this repertoire.

Familiar Tools in Action #1: Listing (page 90)

Teacher: "Let's make a list of all the kinds of animals we can think of. Working in teams, you have exactly 3 minutes to create as long a list as you can. Ready, go."

As students create the list, either in small groups or whole class, student engagement is high because the task is open-ended, nonthreatening, and playful. The teaching objective might be to use the list to practice alphabetizing or classifying; or to lead in to a writing assignment (e.g., "Write a paragraph titled 'My Favorite Animal'"). Or practice using a dictionary, encyclopedia, or Google search to find out more about one of the animals. Or do all of these.

The analysis: Your time is scarce. Using the Listing tool means you did not have to photocopy anything or write anything on the whiteboard. Since students will be engaged with the task, you do not have to force their compliance by collecting and grading their lists. The students will be efficiently accessing prior knowledge regarding animals, and simultaneously accessing positive emotions. The collaborative nature allows less able and less motivated learners to still benefit from the knowledge and enthusiasm of their peers. The force of this pleasant emotion will carry over into the academic task that follows—alphabetizing, classifying, writing, etc. In one brief 3-minute activity, you have facilitated student engagement and accessing of prior knowledge, while creating minimal work for yourself.

Furthermore, within this playful context is a *time constraint* ("... you have exactly 3 minutes"). When used appropriately in a nonthreatening manner, time constraints can be very motivating to children. Something to think about ... kids can fill up extra time the way we fill up storage space; if you are given more storage space, you somehow manage to degenerate in your inefficiency until the space is filled up. Constraints not only prompt efficient use of the resource (i.e., time, space, etc.), but give you a runner's high from the effort and talent applied in the very act of being efficient. You might even say that many students can be catalyzed into a peak performance state merely by getting them to choose to speed up.

Familiar Tools in Action #2: Search Tasks (page 96)

Search tasks—or scavenger hunts—are very quick and easy to construct. Here are some math worksheet examples spanning a variety of grade levels: "Find something in the room that is (1) less than an inch long, (2) 10–15 inches long, (3) rectangular, (4) triangular, (5) more than 20 square inches in area and less than 50 square inches, (6) 30–70 cubic centimeters in volume."

Analysis: Because your time is scarce, it is vital that you be able to create math practice problems designed specifically for your students, and to do it easily and quickly within 5–10 minutes. This is far more effective than depending upon commercial curriculum materials. In this *search task* example, you can include the exact concepts you taught, and at the level that is appropriate, with both easier and more challenging items. The children will enjoy being out of their seats and working collaboratively and with greater success, and you will have time to interact with the students who most need your help.

▸ Additional Tools

Here are several more familiar tools to look into.

Anecdotes	page 16
Scenarios	page 17
Systems design	page 47
"What's my rule" games	page 79
Interviews	page 38
Wait time	page 44
Turn to a neighbor	page 71

■ WHY A REPERTOIRE?

The concept of repertoire is so important to teaching, yet it has not gained much attention. To have a larger instructional repertoire is simply to have ready command of more options. You will find that this gives you more freedom, more power to inspire, more enjoyment, and more success.

As your repertoire grows, so too will student success. *You will be more successful working less, not more.* Because the kids will be on your side, they will want to please you more. They'll persevere because it's more interesting to them, and they are confident they will succeed. The more you develop your repertoire, the more natural, spontaneous, and enjoyable your teaching becomes.

You may be investing the same amount of time, perhaps even more *time*, but you will be working *less*. When your teaching day exhausts you, it is partly due to the amount of time you are spending with schoolwork, but more so, due to the stress you are enduring. Your goal is not to strictly minimize the time you invest, but rather to minimize any energy that teaching drains from you. The more you enjoy your teaching, the more you are in control. And by being in control, you will find yourself investing time as an educator purely because it is so satisfying! Almost like a paid hobby! (Well, maybe that's a bit *too* much of a stretch.)

Here are seven key reasons to develop your repertoire.

Efficiency

Repertoires enable you to be more efficient; when you have the right tool for the job, you get more results for the time and effort invested. This in turn leaves you with more energy at the end of the day, more time to relax or to connect with a student, more downtime to collect your thoughts and to be present in the moment.

Versatility

Resources for educators have become increasingly specialized. Thus, there are books for building kids' self-esteem. And there are books for classroom management techniques, for teaching reading or math, and for fostering thinking skills. Books for faster learners, slower learners. Fortunately, many superb teaching tools are broadly applicable to a wide range of these objectives. Again, the versatility of many tools enables you to be more efficient.

Accessibility

An organized repertoire optimally provides structure and guidance to your cognitive knowledge of teaching. A repertoire is really a collection of autopilot routines that your brain can access with minimal effort. It is the autopilot part of your teaching that makes possible your growth from novice to expert (National Research Council, 2000). Experts have a vast autopilot repertoire that novices cannot possibly have yet accumulated. A repertoire provides an organizational structure so that your brain more quickly and reliably accesses your instructional knowledge. It is comparable to the efficiency you have in your kitchen by keeping all silverware in one drawer, and plates and bowls in another. You can find things faster. Likewise, your brain more reliably finds your instructional knowledge when it is cognitively organized into a generalized repertoire.

Orchestration

It is the orchestration that separates the expert educator from the novice. And this orchestration is hindered if your thinking is too absorbed with the components of the lesson. You want your attention directed toward the orchestration, because unless you have a classroom of homogeneous and perfect kids, *masterful orchestration is the highest-level skill that identifies one as an extraordinary educator!*

Fluid Organization

Each teaching moment is unique, with so many constantly changing factors, many of which are beyond your control. When you have a solid command of a versatile repertoire, you can more readily take advantage of teachable moments. Master the art of being simultaneously both organized and flexible—this is fluid organization.

Alignment with Diverse Models and Research

A large instructional repertoire will find long-term relevance across a great range of teaching models and educational research. There are many tools that mesh simultaneously with what we know from cognitive psychology, multiple intelligences, brain research, learning styles, performance assessment, gifted education, learning disabilities, leadership research, and many other domains.

Student Learning

A well-developed repertoire improves student learning. You can relatively instantly design, modify, and individualize lessons. You can quickly respond to those teachable moments because your repertoire enables you to be more nimble. You can reach more of the diversity of student abilities, interests, temperaments, multiple-intelligence talents, and learning styles. In less time, not more time, you will have students succeeding more than before.

■ THREE USES OF YOUR REPERTOIRE

Each tool in your repertoire can be applied to one or more of three strategic areas. As always, time is scarce, and you want to get the most mileage from the least effort. So the ideal is to achieve all three with the same tool. Here are the three.

Motivational Power

Your effectiveness arises at least in part from your ability to inspire in children their enjoyment of learning, their positive self-beliefs, and their willingness to be cooperative and responsible. When children desire to be around you, to be in your classroom, you have far greater power to affect their lives in positive ways.

Positive Classroom Climate

You are most effective when you build trusting relationships within your classroom. The positive feel of a classroom is a very potent foundation for learning.

Academic Learning Outcomes

And obviously, you are there to teach specific content and skills—the explicit and assessed outcomes within math, reading, writing, science, and others.

■ YOUR REPERTOIRE'S THREE USES IN ACTION: THE "NEAT STUFF BOX"

Collect in a box a variety of interesting, novel, and personal items. I call it a "neat stuff box." You call it what you like. Photos of you as a child or teen are a great item to toss in the box. So is the broken pocket calculator with the back taken off to see the "guts." Hey, the younger the kids you teach, the easier it is to find items that are interesting.

Fifth grade teacher: "I was looking through my old photo album, and found some pictures of me when I was ten; you should see the clothes I was wearing; and my hair style . . ." (Students will of course be interested, and you now have more power to inspire than you did 30 seconds ago.) "We have 20 minutes left before lunch. If you get your math problems finished a little early, we should still have a few minutes left for seeing the pictures." Now, let's analyze this brief episode.

This will be a bit of arithmetic, so follow closely. Basically, when your students see a payoff in terms of something fun, you have more power to motivate them. So perhaps now they will get 30 minutes of work done in 20 minutes, creating 10 minutes that did not even exist before. From those 10 minutes that you miraculously created, you invest 5 of those minutes back into the fun activity. (Still following me on the arithmetic?) Thus, sharing the photo and talking about your childhood did not really take up any time because, really, you created time where no time had even existed.

With something as simple as this neat stuff box, students will be enjoying your class more, which is nearly always a plus. You are investing in relationship building, which is one of the most essential factors for success with your at-risk students and your chronic underachievers.

You will smile and laugh more, which has innumerable positive consequences both inside and outside of school. It improves your nonverbal body language with the kids, reduces your stress level, and improves the quality of your sleep. So you will be in a more energized state for tomorrow.

Interestingly, by doing nothing more strenuous than taking a photo out of a box, you have accomplished two chief uses of your repertoire—positive classroom climate and inspirational power. Let's go for the third—academic learning outcomes. Apply a small bit of creative thinking, really not much creativity at all is required, and the academic connections fall into place.

Writing example: You share your photo . . . which leads to talking about how much fun it is to interview someone about his or her life and childhood . . . which leads to your writing assignment where students interview a parent of other adult about that person's childhood.

Social studies example: You share your photo . . . which leads to talking about how much things have changed . . . which leads to kids guessing which technologies you had or didn't have as a child (e.g., color TV, computers, cell phone, electricity) . . . which leads to a unit you are teaching on technology . . . which leads to each student picking a technology to research for a project.

In review, the three uses of your repertoire are all brought together simply and elegantly with your "neat stuff box." It took minimal effort or time to pull out a photo; nudge the kids into working faster (i.e., power); laugh with them for a few minutes about your silly hairstyle, and how different you looked (i.e., positive classroom climate); and lead seamlessly into the their writing assignment (i.e., academic learning outcome).

This "neat stuff" can be shared with the whole class, or alternatively, you can pick items specifically to share with particular students. This one-to-one sharing can be even more powerful than sharing with the whole class.

Ah, if only teaching could always be this easy! These examples are not meant to impress you, or to present a simplistic and idealistic notion of what goes on in a classroom. No, it's more like this—*by consciously applying these win-win tools, your teaching can be easier than it is.*

Section 2
The Tools

The tools in these chapters are exceedingly adaptable and versatile. Use them often and they will become increasingly automatic. And that's the point—for your repertoire to be a spontaneous expression of your wisdom and personality, and attuned with those teachable moments. You will find, also, that most of these require minimal preparation and can produce extraordinary results.

Chapter 2
The Power of Relationship

> Your success as an educator is more dependent on positive, caring, trustworthy, relationships than on any skill, idea, tip, or tool in this book.
> *Eric Jensen (1988, 139)*

It has been stated many times that teaching is about creating relationships. Two of the tools in this chapter—one-to-one time and strategic irrelevance—are exceedingly effective and enjoyable, and require minimal time.

■ ONE-TO-ONE TIME

This is the very simple technique of interacting with a single student for generally a few seconds or a few minutes. The effectiveness of one-to-one time can sometimes be instant and dramatic. I have seen students' behaviors, work habits, and attitudes do a complete turnaround after a mere 5-minute meeting with them. I am not alone—many educators tell me the same thing.

Even if dramatic improvements do not materialize, at worst you lost 5 minutes. *There are very, very few investments of your time that present such an opportunity for results with so little teacher effort.*

Find time during the day or week to interact with students individually. This could be casually during lunch, after school, in the hall, or during a hands-on lesson. But be sure you are in a decent mood!

For some of you, this one-to-one time is something you have been doing automatically and intuitively for years. You'll need no coaching from me. For other teachers, the power of one-to-one time is something you have not yet internalized. In that case, you might want to start with those students with whom you already have good rapport.

Your goal here is to just be physically and emotionally present with a student. Enjoy their company. Talk about something of mutual interest. Listen to the student; do not judge or critique, just listen to the feelings as well as the words. And in many cases, it may not even be appropriate to bring in any topic related to school. Maybe all you need to do is enjoy the interaction.

If you do not have rapport with a particular student, you will want to try the Strategic Irrelevance strategy that follows.

Whether your one-to-one time works or not depends far less on the words, but instead on the child's perception of you—"Are you really enjoying this time with me? Do you actually care about me? Are you actually listening instead of judging? Do I feel safe to share my feelings and thoughts?"

A teacher in one of my workshops wrote, "My main focus was to increase one-to-one time. This has improved my classes a great deal. I have had contact with the underachievers first and I've seen a general improvement in my class. The improvement was mostly in attitude and attentiveness, not in quality or quantity of work. However, I am very happy with what I've seen so far." This experience is typical. To win students over effectively—to build a relationship that is not adversarial—is a first step toward academic improvement.

A few more ideas for one-to-one time . . .

Just Noticing to Build Rapport

"I noticed your new bicycle." "I noticed you smiling before class." "I noticed how much effort you put into your essay." (Adapted from Fay and Funk, 1998)

Focusing on a Strength

You want your students to "own" their talents and successes, rather than depend on your praise day after day. Identify one or two strengths of a student. Each time that student exhibits one of these strengths, notice this with the student one-to-one as soon afterward as possible. Do this throughout the school year.

Extending Learning; Talented, Motivated Students

Ask, "What kinds of books are your favorites?" "Would you like to continue this science experiment at home?" "Wow, you did great on the math today—here's a really fun and challenging one to try."

Getting Feedback Regarding Student Attitudes

Ask individual students, "How is school going for you this year?" "What makes a good teacher?" "What was the most fun this year?" "When have you made your best efforts to learn this year? Why?"

STRATEGIC IRRELEVANCE

You have all used this strategy. Sometimes, the best way to connect with a student is to do or say something that has absolutely nothing to do with school or your teacher role. Thus, it is irrelevant, and therefore feels safer or more novel to many students. You have all noticed the captivating effect of irrelevance when you have spontaneously shared some completely pointless anecdote. You have probably shared with students how you spilled your coffee or your alarm didn't go off in the morning or your 3 year old had her birthday.

Furthermore, by being "irrelevant" at strategic times, you can better reach students that have negative or indifferent attitudes toward particular subject areas, toward school in general, or toward you.

Examples: I gave an old fishing rod to a student who loves fishing. I listened to one of my barely passing life science students talk about how much she loved young children. I gave a polished beach rock to a student.

For various reasons, many students erect walls to keep us out of their personal space. For example, you ask low-achieving students why they don't have their math homework done, and they shrug, or say it's stupid, or the usual "I don't know." They have their defenses up. Your very proximity stresses them. Subconsciously, their brains withdraw from the potential threat to their safety. They have little intention of reflecting on your question, or responding openly.

With these students, focusing on the problem—whether the problem is academic or behavioral—is often unsuccessful because the foundation of trust and safety is not there. You need to create a bond with students before they will allow you into their personal emotional space. The bond is a pre-condition for any hope of a solution that the student will own. This is where strategic irrelevance comes in.

If you do not yet have a bond—some rapport or trust—with a student, initiate interaction via some avenue that has nothing to do with school. These students are expecting to feel uncomfortable when you are near them. Instead, ask who won the football game. Or if they think it will rain. In the lunch line, ask whether the French fries are any good. Or forget being verbal at all, and just do something silly with the student. Or give the student a responsibility that communicates your trust. Or walk out to the basketball court when the student is practicing with the team. While munching on cashews, say "These are my favorite nuts; would you like some?"

Or share something from your "neat stuff box."

Keep in mind that if your irrelevant gesture is perceived as being out-of-character, the student may just view you as being peculiar, or worse, sneaky and manipulative. Therefore, you want to break down barriers with students by (1) being yourself, (2) communicating caring and respect, and (3) referring *not at all* to any problems. The interaction should be kept simple, brief, and pleasant. Nothing profound.

Example: I had a 7th grader, Carl, who was a slower learner and feeling frustrated in class. As a busy teacher, I hadn't taken time to bond with Carl as an individual. I saw little of his strengths, and much of his academic weaknesses. For Carl, school was a place of feeling dumb, struggling, and being stressed.

I did know that Carl loved riding his mountain bike. One day after school, he was out in the parking lot with his bike and some friends. I challenged him to a bike ride around the lot. He liked the idea. I borrowed a bike from his friend, I raced my very best, though Carl had far more coordination, and I lost the race. Needless to say, Carl was pleased.

Yet we both won for the following reasons. The race was totally irrelevant to school, which is why it appealed to Carl. However, it was very relevant to enabling him to demonstrate an area of talent and competency. And he achieved this in front of friends. And he showed that he's better than I! Meanwhile, I communicated nonverbally that I enjoy him, that I recognize he has talent. I modeled the willingness to try something I wasn't yet good at. And the laughter and aerobic exercise was great for both of us! I was able to get exercise, have fun, and bond with one or more students, without it costing me anything.

Whether it is the following day, or the next week, I can now approach Carl during class and ask how he's doing with the essay we're writing. And for the first time, Carl allows me to help him. He no longer responds, "This is stupid." Instead he asks, "Can you help me with this paragraph?"

Whole group strategic irrelevance: "Who in our class has the best match between their eye color and their socks?" "Whoever lost a tooth the most recently is first in line to lunch." One teacher shared with me that she has been talking to her students more about sports, and now they have been more willing to complete their work.

■ STUDENTS TEACHING TEACHERS

Be sure that at times during the school year, the children will teach you something. Make yourself accessible to these many opportunities that spontaneously arise. For example . . . a child can teach you how to skateboard . . . the words to a song . . . a dance move . . . how to play chess . . . how to recognize that her dog is a Labradoodle and not just a poodle . . . what attaches to this particular Lego piece . . . why a certain animated character is the best in the whole world.

■ DURATION VERSUS IMPACT

Remember . . . the impact of an experience on the life of a child may extend far beyond its brief duration. What you want is impact. Many brief experiences in life carry lasting emotional impact—for example, a hug, or a compliment from someone you admire. And, unfortunately, being teased, insulted, or embarrassed.

Something you might share or teach may last but a few moments, yet the positive effects can have repercussions in student behavior and attitude throughout the day, sometimes the year, and occasionally for the child's life. There's no limit—everything is interconnected—and joy and caring are contagious.

■ PERSONALIZING TECHNIQUES

This assortment of strategies can add that personal touch to your teaching.

"Good Luck"

Teacher: "Boys and girls, this next math problem is a fun one, but it's also a challenging one. Turn to someone near you and say, "Good luck."

Many kids love this. In a number of classrooms, the good luck, which can be accompanied by a handshake, develops into a spontaneous habit of the students. What a joyful habit for students to develop!

And when students wish each other good luck, they are creating the positive self-talk that influences effort and success. One teacher is convinced that the spelling scores improved dramatically after her 2nd graders started wishing each other good luck before their quizzes.

Personalizing the Classroom

For example, give children a small section of wall space for their own decorating. Or perhaps a child might bring in a small plant, create a "welcome" sign for the door, or help select appropriate CDs for silent reading or indoor recess.

Personalizing Classroom Discussion

Use your students' names in lessons and examples. Instead of "Imagine someone was in a forest, and . . ." say "Imagine Clara was in the forest behind her house, and . . ."

Personalizing Assignments

When students are investigating a topic, whether trees, or literature, encourage more ownership by having them label their assignment "My Tree," or "My Story." Simple, and it works.

Secrets

Many children love secrets about their teacher. Example: "If we can get our work done 5 minutes early, I have a secret to tell you, if you promise not to tell anyone." Then go ahead and tell them how you always wanted a dog, or something silly or embarrassing you did, or . . .

Chapter 3
Visual and Personalized Learning

Of the many attributes of an experience that might engage a child's mind, two especially powerful ones are brought together in this chapter—making it visual, and bringing the child into that visual picture.

■ ANECDOTES—PAINT A PICTURE, AND PERSONALIZE IT

An anecdote is any short, engaging, personalized account of a life experience. A good anecdote paints a mental picture. And it personalizes the concepts. Furthermore, anecdotes bring out your real voice, not your teacher voice. (Very few people enjoy the "teacher voice.") This is an extraordinarily powerful combination, and probably explains why *anecdotes are the tool most frequently used by the best speakers and presenters.*

A good anecdote grabs students' attention, connects content to life, and builds relationships. All of us have an abundant source of anecdotes packed into our life experiences. All it takes is to package an incident in your life as an informal story. Then find a time to present it. Learn to value these stories. And let them be a natural extension of many of your lessons.

Kids just love to hear your real voice. It doesn't sound like a lecture—or even like school—and that alone will entice them. With a good story, the kids connect with your authentic self.

Few instructional tools are as versatile. Use them to start lessons, as well as for review or closure. Anecdotes are well suited to connecting with at-risk children one-to-one. And, in all cases, anecdotes take such minimal preparation, and there's no paperwork to grade.

Some ways to use anecdotes include the following:

- *To start a lesson:* Let the story lead naturally into your lesson topic. Life Science: Tell about the time you got food poisoning, and lead into your unit on bacteria. Primary: Tell about something you lost, and lead into having the students write their names in their books.
- *To teach concepts:* You can do it one of two ways. Either state the lesson's concept, then use an anecdote as an example. Or share the story, then state the concept that supports it.
- *To reinforce learning days or weeks later:* Use anecdotes as engaging examples to practice concepts already taught. The visual, story-like nature of the anecdote facilitates student comprehension and retention.
- *To build rapport and team spirit:* Students love learning about their teachers' lives. A few good stories here and there can really spice up the day and create more positive feelings. Your students will appreciate seeing you as a human being and not just as a teacher.
- *To improve classroom management and resolve conflicts:* Present the anecdote as a problem to be solved. It might, for example, be a story of a classroom issue or problem from a past year. Ask students what they would have done in your situation.
- *To change attitudes and habits*: Perhaps the most important use of anecdotes is to visually and emotionally connect children to the attitudes and habits they most need to learn. Thus, find your own life stories that teach such things as . . . persevering, dealing with a bully, being responsible, being a friend, cleaning up your messes, working as a team, believing in yourself.

Maintain a stack of file cards, each with a brief reminder of an anecdote that teaches one of the above attitudes and habits. Over the course of a school year, you will spontaneously recall more and more of these stories from your own life. The file card system will be a resource for each year that follows.

■ SCENARIOS

Scenarios are hypothetical scenes. Like anecdotes, scenarios paint a picture and personalize it. Nearly all teachers can use this tool, and use it often! It is one of the best instructional tools around. You may not be able to take field trips to the past, to the future, or to a distant place, but you can take kids there nonetheless with a scenario.

Social studies, language arts: "You and your family just moved to another country. You decide the country where you are living. Tell me what it feels like. Is it exciting? Or scary? Or both? Write a letter to a friend back home."

Here are several benefits of scenarios:

- Scenarios help students escape from their standard thinking patterns. They facilitate creative and lateral thinking by placing us in new situations requiring fresh thought, rather than rote responses.
- Scenarios enable students to better personalize an experience or concept, thus leading to higher levels of participation, active thinking, and retention. This is extremely important for students whose learning style thrives on that personal connection.
- Scenarios enable teachers to explore an extraordinarily wide range of topics, both realistic and hypothetical, simple to complex, across any subject area with any grade level.
- Scenarios require minimal prep time to develop, and can be incorporated at numerous stages in a lesson—as motivational lead-ins, discussion questions, review, or as test questions.

A number of general examples are given below, followed by numerous variations.

Language arts, self-awareness: "You are going to live in a lighthouse on a small, uninhabited island for one year, and you can only bring 5 items with you (besides clothes, food, water). Which five would you take along? (e.g., boat, radio, a dog, books, television, telephones, a friend, stereo, new clothes). Explain your choices."

"You are now an adult, and have your very own 8-year-old son or daughter. What are the five most important things you will to tell your child?"

Middle school social studies: "You are a congressman who will be voting next week on a gun control bill. How will you vote, and how will you explain your choice to your constituents?"

"You have won an exciting 2-week vacation to one of the European countries we have learned about this quarter. It is your job to plan the itinerary."

Math: "You have $100 to spend on any of the toys in these advertisements. Decide which you would buy, and how much money you would have left. If you want to be even more advanced, I can help you figure out sales tax."

"You are creating a recipe to make three servings of 'spicy, sweet, fried, yogurt, worm crunch.' Make a list of ingredients with the quantity of each, and the cost to make it. We will have a master list of food costs up here on the wall."

Nutrition: "You are in charge of planning the school lunch menu for 1 month. In groups of three, plan the menu, applying what we know about nutrition, and explain how you did it."

"What-if" Scenarios

"What-ifs" are very popular for good reason. They require minimal teacher preparation, and facilitate open-ended higher-level thinking. Have students create their own what-ifs to stimulate student ownership.

Reality what-ifs: These prompt awareness of alternatives.

> "What if we do our spelling practice during the 10 minutes just before lunch?"
> "What if the U.S. Congress is controlled by Democrats instead of Republicans?"
> "What if we had five periods per day instead of six?"
> "What if parents started to genetically design their children before birth to make them more intelligent, healthier, and physically more attractive?"
> "What if all land on this planet were considered public, i.e., there was no such thing as privately owned real estate?"

Creativity what-ifs: Facilitate humor, cooperation, and playful participation, as well as creative thinking. These are good starting points for creative writing assignments, or critical thinking analyses.

> "What if you could spend as much money as you wanted for a day?"
> "What if you were the richest person in the world?"
> "What if you and everyone else were allowed only a certain number of words that they could speak during their lifetime?"
> "What if you never had to go to sleep?" "What if you were ten-feet tall?"

Self-awareness what-ifs: These may be serious or humorous in tone.

> "What if you could be better at one thing; what would it be, and how would that change your life?"
> "What if you could see yourself 10 years from now; what do you think you'll see? What would you like to see?"
> "What if your house (or dog, TV, etc.) could speak—what would it say to you?"

Academic applications: Extend your scenarios much further into your academic content. For example, assign students to create a brainstormed list or mind map of twenty possible direct and indirect outcomes from the scenario. They can share responses orally, in writing, with pictures, or even with songs. They can do this as a whole class or in small groups. Lead from these to writing essays, making presentations, conducting debates, interviewing experts, or researching the question further using the Internet.

Time-Travel Scenarios

Scenarios allow unlimited movement not only in space but also in time. You can travel to the past or the future. Individuals from the past or the future can travel to the present. Here are several variations to get you started. Finally . . . a way to make the abstract notion of history more concrete, visual, and experiential!

▶ *Time Travel: Past to Present*

This historical visit enables students to better comprehend history and culture, to step outside their own thinking and cultural conditioning, and to examine things that we so often take for granted.

"Imagine various persons from history visiting our classroom (or our community, or country). What would surprise them most? Least? Become that person (e.g., George Washington)—you have been invited to write an article for the school newspaper. What will you write?"

▶ *Time Travel: Present to Past*

"You are traveling back in time. You can change one thing. What time period will you go back to, and what will you change?"

"You are on the Mayflower. Write a journal entry to a relative back home, telling them what you brought with you, what you are looking forward to, what worries you."

▶ *Time Travel: Present to Future*

"You are living in the year 2100, and are reading an account of the history of the U.S. (or world) from 2000 to 2100 (100 years). Describe that history as (1) you expect it to read, and (2) you would hope it to be." Students may focus on population changes, technological advances, political or economic changes, lifestyle changes, etc. Ask "Does technology solve problems, or create them?"

"You are 100 years old. Describe how people are different. What new careers will there be? What will people do for fun? How will each of the following be similar to or different from today: technology, education, houses, transportation?"

Best-Case/Worst-Case Scenarios

Start with either a real or imaginary situation. Then brainstorm best-case outcomes in one list—or mind map—while generating a worst-case collection of outcomes in the other.

Many of us get locked into sets of perceptions from which it is difficult to escape. Best- and worst-case scenarios can specifically redirect learners' attention to possibilities that might otherwise be overlooked. Thus, a pessimistic person is forced to search for the positive, and a naively optimistic attitude becomes a bit more enlightened as to the potential drawbacks.

Examples: Do a best-case/worst-case analysis of allowing gum-chewing in school, legalizing a drug, or holding children accountable for making an effort to learn.

Self-esteem, goal setting: Many students see a glass half empty; your job is to help them see that it is also half-full. Facilitate a best-case/worst-case discussion of "trying something that you're not good at."

Scenario Challenges

Combine creative writing, self-awareness, and sharing. Create a hypothetical bet to place students in a novel situation. This novelty motivates your learners toward new patterns of thinking and awareness.

"If someone bet you $100,000 to live off in the wilderness by yourself for 1 year, would you do it? What skills would you want to have? What would you want to bring with you?"

Our brain's left-mode continually tries to reduce all experience to what is already known, labeled, and categorized. Novel situations jolt our left-mode out of its rote, autopilot thoughts and perceptions. This newness stimulates the mind—especially the "right mode"—into active engagement.

Scenario Headlines

Start with hypothetical headlines. These can be local or personal in scope; they can focus on your particular community or school, or on individual students. As an interesting self-awareness exercise, let students write up positive headlines, placing themselves as the main character.

Self-awareness and esteem: "You are on the front page of our school newspaper next month. Write the headline and the article." (Or for younger children, draw the picture.)

Global issues: "Based upon our readings and discussion, write an article for the following imaginary news headline dated 2025. The headline reads, "Coastal cities need more federal aid to battle rising sea level."

Current issues, biology, health: The headline reads, "All research funding is cut for medical technologies aimed at keeping elderly alive." Or you might try this headline: "Genetic engineers create first perfect baby."

Scenario Predictions

Present your students with a scenario, and have them make predictions. Here is a part of an example assignment I used for 7th grade social studies:

> For each of the country descriptions below, what reasonable assumptions or predictions might you make? What might the economy be like? Is the country rich or poor? Why? What are the most important ways people might earn a living? Do you think tourism might be important? Why or why not? Is the country probably a peaceful one, or is there tension or even a civil war? What other ideas or predictions did you come up with? Is there a real country that might be similar to the scenario?
>
> Country #1: a group of tropical islands isolated in the middle of the ocean, and inhabited by a native culture that lived here prior to arrival of the first European explorers. There is some good agricultural land, some good fishing, no mining.
>
> Country #2: a country at a subtropical latitude with a very dry climate. There is a small population and an abundance of petroleum reserves.

■ PROPS

A prop is anything that can be used to attract the students' eyes, and thus their attention. Vision is often our primary sense, a dominant form of sensory input, providing the basis for much of our learning. Where our eyes go, our thoughts and minds will often follow.

For example, a glass of saltwater can be used to begin discussion of the oceans; holding an apple can focus the students' attention on a discussion of food; and a sectioned orange may provide a concrete model for discussion of fractions.

Add novelty: Have a puppet lecture to your primary classroom. This adds both a visual element and a degree of novelty—learning will be enhanced as long as the novelty does not distract too much from the intended learning.

Use colors, shapes, sizes: Enhance learning by connecting concepts with visual experiences—use colors to emphasize concepts by underlining or outlining in color. Vary the sizes of words.

Use location: Stand in different parts of the room for particular concepts you are teaching. For example, stand in one part of the room while giving examples of nouns, and in another part of the room while discussing adjectives.

Vision is one of our dominant senses. If your students' eyes are not focused on your intended learning, then their eyes may be preoccupied with what is outside the window, or the ant crawling across the floor, or the doodling on their desk.

■ Packaging with Essential Questions

If you would rule the world quietly, you must keep it amused.
Ralph Waldo Emerson

Don't be deceived into thinking that students *should* want to attend school, *should* want to learn, *should* want to please their teacher. Because then you might think it's *not* your responsibility to "package" your lessons the way an author packages a novel, an artist packages a painting, a company packages a product.

"Essential questions" are one exceedingly simple and powerful technique. Decide what big questions or goals would connect with students' lives and can guide your curriculum for a week, month, or year. Then package these questions so that students will want the learning, the skills, the competency. The Coalition of Essential Schools suggests just such a conceptualization should drive your curriculum (Steinberg and Cushman, 1999).

For example, in middle school social studies: "This year we will be learning about different cultures and the history of different places. The big question is this: 'What, if anything, can we learn from people and from history to make your lives better?'" Then each assignment, reading, and lesson every day will at some point return to this question.

Language arts example: "Everything we read this year will be with the intent of answering this question: 'What does this literature tell me about myself, my values, my personality, my goals?'"

■ Packaging through Humor and Personal Connection: Name the Day or Week

You and the kids can title almost anything—and this title can have a mnemonic purpose in helping children to recall prior learning. "Week of the Fire Drills." "Day of the Teddy Bear." "Endless Rain." "Air-Conditioner Broken." You can create a number line recording the school days, and tape notes to whichever days have the distinction of a name. As the school year progresses, these names become "handles" that prompt students' recall of their learning during that time. Get creative: "We-Love-Adverbs Day." Humor, laughter, and personalized mnemonics create community as well as retention.

■ VISUALIZATION AND IMAGERY

We think in images, not in sentences. Just try to remember a recent ten-word sentence you've heard. To visualize in the broadest sense is nothing more than to engage visual processing in the brain.

The many variations of visualization and imagery all capitalize on the propensity for human beings to learn readily via the visual parts of their brains. In those cases where the content or skills to be learned cannot be physically presented to the students, visualization can substitute for the real thing. We can visualize with our eyes either open or shut. Having students close their eyes to visualize helps to avoid external visual distractions. The simplest visualization technique is to preface a lesson with "Picture this . . ." or "Imagine . . ."

Whether the visual experiencing is accomplished via external reality or internal imaging, you will be able to facilitate more effective learning, especially with complex concepts. Presenting effective visualizations may take some trial and error with your students—but it's a technique well worth trying.

Positive outcomes of visualization/imagery include the following:

- *Learning:* Improve attention, whole-brain thinking, and retention. The nerve pathways involved in the learning can be reinforced via visualization even in the absence of actual physical practice. For example, basketball players visualizing their shooting actually improve in shooting.
- *Enjoyment, success, and self-concept:* Enhance positive self-perceptions and positive expectations. Facilitate relaxation and stress reduction. Encourage humor, joy and sharing.

Imagery/visualization exercises come in a wide variety of forms, depending upon one's goals, the age and prior experiences of the individuals, and the nature of the content. Here are a few.

Practical/Informational Imagery

This form of imagery stimulates learning and retention of information or skills. For example, ask students to imagine the steps in today's science lab procedure, as you describe it. These visualizations generally will work fine with students' eyes open. "Visualize being a molecule in a cracker as it goes into your mouth, gets chewed and swallowed, flows through your digestive tract, all the while being acted upon by enzymes."

Creative Imagery

"Imagine a herd of cows coming into the gym and tap-dancing during an assembly."

Language arts, drama: These fanciful visualizations are lead-ins to creative writing, drama, artwork, creative thinking, and laughter.

Relaxation Imagery

Use imagery to ease tension or to calm nervous energy: "You are traveling to a distant, beautiful place, full of color, delicious foods, and soft music, your body becoming weightless and fully relaxed."

Learning how to relax, by imagery or other means, is a life skill that benefits everyone. You may find it appropriate when working with troubled students, immediately before a test, or when students need to be calmed down.

Success Imagery

Success imagery stimulates self-awareness, positive expectations of oneself, and personal empowerment. Some of these are more effectively accomplished one-to-one with a particular student, rather than as a whole group.

Self-esteem: "You are now filling a garbage can with all the bad things that have happened to you. Now dump that garbage can."

Reinforcement of learning: "Visualize and feel a time when you succeeded at something in school. Decide you will succeed like that again."

Self-awareness, goal setting: "Imagine being any person you could be—what does it feel like, what are you thinking?"

College and career goals: "Picture yourself as a success 3 years from now in college."

Cooperation: "Imagine yourself as a wonderful person. You're kind and generous with others, and your friends love you for it."

■ OBSERVATION CENTERS

These may include an aquarium or terrarium, classroom pets, magnets, potted plants, or weather instruments.

Optimal learning occurs when children have abundant sensory exposure to diverse experiences over extended periods of time. These on-going centers can provide students with motivational, concrete raw material from which learning can take place. This is true of students at any age—I noticed repeatedly with my own high school students that they just loved looking at things that were interesting to them.

Concept learning: The observation centers are especially powerful when you facilitate and focus student observations to align with your curriculum. "Do the magnets pick up all of the objects, or just some of them?"

Math: "What percent of the day does the hamster sleep?" Make a graph of the growth of the hamster, or plant.

Language arts: The presence of the pet, or magnets, in the classroom will motivate the children that much more when reading or writing about them.

Student self-reliance and leadership: Have one or more students in charge of taking care of the hamster, researching pet foods, or maintaining an observation log.

■ VISUAL ENHANCEMENT

Make use of different colors to enhance the learning of a skill—e.g. learning to read—or to further motivate visual learners.

Help students who are having trouble learning words phonetically. Write each letter of the word in a different color. Then have students close their eyes and visualize the word, as well as hearing it silently without moving their lips.

And, finally, tell students to write the word several times with their eyes still closed.

> - *Organizational skills:* To help maintain organization of materials, students can color code their subjects, the locations where classroom supplies are kept, or their student tasks.
> - *Language arts:* Color code parts of speech; the rhyming parts of a series of words; the author, title, publisher; the main character, supporting characters, and plot.
> - *Visual play:* Incorporate "rainbows" into assignments. Students can make each page of a workbook a different color or each letter of their name a different color.

Highlighting and Color Coding

Provide felt-tipped highlighting markers to enhance motivation and learning in many students. The fluorescent ones are especially exciting!

Main ideas: When we highlight text, we often read it more carefully to know what to highlight. When we review later, the marked text leaps out at us. Thus, highlighting may facilitate original learning as well as subsequent practice. Open-note tests are very highly recommended as an effective means for providing students with practical experience at note taking and highlighting.

Feedback, ownership: Encourage students to highlight parts of their assignments. Here's a way to get kids to take more ownership and give you valuable feedback for assessment purposes: "Highlight the math problems you found easiest." "Highlight the part of your essay which you believe is the best." "Highlight the words where you are not sure of the spelling."

Math: Children highlight addition signs in green, subtraction signs in red. Highlight the hundreds, tens, and ones places in different colors.

Motivation and reward: "When you finish your first five math problems, you may come up and get a highlighter to finish the rest."

Calligraphy

Combine art with writing! Some of your more visual and tactile learners may love calligraphy. The act of doing calligraphy stimulates an increased sense of pride in the quality and neatness of one's work. A student who is not in the mood for writing may be motivated to write when handed a calligraphy pen. It is quite possible that calligraphy may help a learner draw upon the brain's right hemisphere during the writing process.

Fine motor skills: For primary students who are gaining increased proficiency with penmanship.

Relaxation: Use calligraphy pens to relax or quiet students, or as an option when a student completes work early.

Language Arts: Create beautiful title pages for essays or reports.

Creativity: You can make some splendid doodle-art.

Chapter 4
Learner-Centered Dialogue

Within your repertoire you want to have strategies and activities that engage kids in conversations that interest them, and that pertain to their world and their concerns. This is learner-centered dialogue. It can happen spontaneously, or as a scheduled part of the day or curriculum.

Students need many, many opportunities to really think about open-ended questions. These enable your students to gain the clarity, purpose, and energy so fundamental to effort, confidence, and success.

Cooperation: "How did it feel when you kids figured out how we can work better as a team, and you didn't need me to make more rules?"

Essay-writing lesson: "Think about stuff that you really enjoy, things that you care about, the most important stuff in your life, your dreams for the future. I want your essays to be something that you feel strongly about."

Behavior problems: During a one-to-one meeting with a student following a discipline problem, ask "What do you propose would be a fair solution." You can involve students in determining consequences.

Beginning of the year: Share with your 7th graders what you liked and disliked about school and what you passionately believe about teaching and learning, and why. Engage them in discussion. What is it they believe and feel about school? Ask "What should be the purpose of education?"

■ CLASSROOM MEETINGS

Scheduled classroom meetings are one very powerful way to foster students' responsibility and ownership. If you've never led a classroom meeting, or you want to pursue it to its fullest potential, you may want to read one or both of the following (listed in the bibliography): *Positive Discipline in the Classroom* by Jane Nelson and *The Soul of Education* by Rachael Kessler. (The first of these has an elementary slant, and the second is decidedly secondary level.)

You will need to establish protocols for setting the agenda and establishing behavioral expectations. Children, even younger ones, can often take on substantial responsibilities with setting the agenda, proposing ideas for classroom problems, and showing a willingness to listen and compromise.

■ Your Repertoire for Learner-Centered Dialogue

There is such a wide spectrum of choices here.

Open-Ended Questions

Maintain a list of questions that you or students generate. Open up a dialogue with one of these questions at a scheduled time each week, or when there are a few spare moments. Possible questions include:

> - "What was the best day of your life?"
> - "What is absolutely the best dessert on this planet?"
> - "What is something unjust that has happened to you?"
> - "If you could meet anyone who ever lived, who would you want to meet?"
> - "What is the funniest thing you ever did?"
> - "What things do you worry about? What problems do you wish you could solve?"
> - "What do you most want to learn?"
> - "What things puzzle you? What are you curious about?"

Values Tasks

Place students in situations where they can explore their values. Try to infuse these reflective/sharing experiences throughout various curriculum areas through the year.

When students explore and respectfully share their preferences and opinions, there are numerous benefits: (1) students' self-concept grows; (2) thinking skills are used; (3) children become aware of, and more accepting of, the various values among their peers; and (4) when emotions are attached to learning, retention is improved.

Language arts: "Write about someone important to you." "List the characters in the novel from your favorite to least favorite, and explain why you rated them that way." "Why do you think the character in the story made that particular choice? What does that tell us about his/her values?"

Assessment: Include questions on your exams such as "Which parts of the chapter did you like more/less? Explain why." "What part(s) of this unit do you think you will use in your life?" (Answers to each of these questions would count as part of the total grade. Accept any legitimate answer.)

Critical thinking: Have students articulate the reasoning behind their opinions. For example, if you ask your class which sports or hobbies are their favorites, you can generate lively discussion by inquiring "Why is that your favorite?"

Rate, Evaluate, Judge (see page 65 for more information)

Children experience more power and control when their opinions are valued. Likewise, when there is more than one right answer, students will engage far more in any discussion.

Valuing student opinions: You might ask students, "Which fast food is the best?" or "Which is better, to be happy or to be wealthy?" "Would you rather have one or two close friends, or be popular with lots of kids?" "Is it more important to be liked by a parent, or by a friend?"

Curriculum connections: Here's a reading example: "How many pages should a good story be? Why do you say that?"

"Put these in order from your favorite to least favorite: ice cream, skateboards, music, summer vacation, your birthday. After you put them in order, it will be interesting for us to hear your ideas why."

Student Self-assessment (see page 68 for more information)

One of the most powerful avenues for improving students' sense of purpose and control is the process of self-assessment. When students have an understanding of what the learning target looks like, and have ownership of that target, their motivation is vastly increased. So is the likelihood that they will be effectively focused on the task. Involve students in discussion of the important criteria.

Teacher: "When we make our posters, what things should count in the grading?"

Recollection Tasks

Direct students' attention to their past. The focus can be either a specific time or event, or a more general recall of any portion of one's life. Recollection is a valuable self-awareness exercise, helping learners to see their lives as a process of change and growth.

For example:

- "Can you remember what you were like a year ago?"
- "Recall the significant or interesting events each year of your life as far back as you can remember."
- "How have your feelings been changing over the last year—feelings toward school, or friends, or other things?" "What things did you like more last year than this year? What things do you like more this year?"

Language arts: Writing is an obvious extension. Consider also using this tool as a lead-in to reading a biography of another. By first drawing children's attention to themselves, your lesson fosters students' early participation and ownership. You can then connect or transfer their thoughts over to a variety of other concepts.

Social studies: See the previous language arts example for biographies. After students reflect on their own lives, ask them how they suspect their childhood compares with that of a particular historical character.

Self-awareness: In September, have students first recollect past school years. They then write predictions for the present year. Collect their predictions; seal them in envelopes. Open and share at the end of the year.

Behavior or attitude problems: "Do you see any repeating patterns here. Think about this past month . . ."

Life skills/careers: An introspective look at one's past experiences and interests plants the seeds for the viable dreams of the future.

■ Your Repertoire for Student Ownership and Dialogue

Here are a variety of ways to invite students into the process of reflecting upon, sharing, and enjoying themselves and their learning.

Unanswered Questions

This is good for nurturing curiosity and inquiry. The kids collaboratively generate and record unanswered questions. The topic can be specifically related to curriculum, or entirely open. Set aside a brief time, such as 5 minutes, or do this as an ongoing list posted on the wall, and add to it throughout the year. Some possible questions include "Where do butterflies go in the rain?" "What makes clouds so puffy?" and "How come parents split up?"

▸ *I Wonder*

This provides a little more structure. Students each finish the stem "I wonder . . ." in relation to the unit just studied. For example, "I wonder what it would be like if dinosaurs were alive today" or "I wonder what caused them to become extinct." This can either be shared orally with children in a circle, in small groups with one child recording, or individually.

Or try an "I wonder" list that arises spontaneously from the children in the course of the day. "I wonder how they make stuffed animals."

Keepers

Keepers are those most significant ideas, concepts, or skills that you want to remember. As closure to a unit, students in small groups or individually can generate keepers. They can be written or shared orally, discussed in small groups or whole class, posted on the wall, or communicated via illustrations.

Question of the Day

Either you or your students can pose a question of the day. You can keep a "class questions list" as students each add their questions. You can organize and classify the questions, maybe even set up a computer database, or send them out over the Internet for answers. Students can rate them from most important to least important, easiest to most difficult. Students can research the answers.

Example: "Is your life mostly what happens to you, or mostly how you react to it?"

All curriculum areas: You can use a question of the day to capture the essential issue or concept that you want your students to learn. It is an excellent way to start and close a major unit or project.

Student-Initiated Statements

This one requires a spirit of community and trust among class members. Provide times when one or more students may address the class with a comment or statement. The rule is that others may not argue or interrupt. Afterwards, students may write their reactions to the statement if they so choose. This opportunity enables students to voice themselves, to be listened to, to express their beliefs without fear of argument.

Shared Feelings

Tune in to how students are feeling toward their task or assignment. One way to do this is simply to ask. Check in with one or two students informally, or ask the entire class.

Students in pairs can share their feelings, whether positive or negative, concerning a particular word or topic. Some possibilities include where you live, school, grownups, favorite pets, or summer.

Creative sharing: Students depict their feelings in writing, in colors, in drawings, in collages. For example, "Write your name the way you are feeling." See if other students can guess each other's feelings from the artwork.

Name Feelings: Do you like your name? What do you like being called—do you have a nickname? Why did your parents give you the name they did?

Partner Introductions

Group students in pairs, preferably randomly. Each student must find out all he or she can about the partner. After 3–5 minutes, each student introduces his or her partner, either to the class or to a small group.

Partner introductions encourage self-awareness, sharing, and listening skills, and enable students and teacher to become better acquainted. After the entire group has been introduced, students can be encouraged to further share something about themselves or ask questions of others.

Primary: Make it more structured, especially for younger children, by providing the children with sample questions to ask of their partner.

Self-questionnaire

Increase students' self-awareness with sentence stems that provide the extra structure needed by many younger children (and older ones as well):

> My favorite activities are . . .
> I like people who . . .
> It is important that . . .
> I'd most like to . . .
> I wish people would . . .

You can write up the questions yourself, or have the students generate the questionnaire. Then share.

Idea Time

Establish "idea time," where you or your students designate an open-ended topic for discussion. For example, the idea time session can be fun games, junk food, wars, television, or smoking cigarettes.

Idea time is exceedingly useful for providing teachers with information on their students' interests, experiences, and misconceptions. Furthermore, idea time enables students to improve their speaking skills, practice listening to others without interrupting, and better connect school with life.

■ AWARENESS OF SELF AND OTHERS

The following activities will remind you of one or more that are already within your repertoire. Several of these can be adapted to connect with various content areas as well.

Focus Words

Each week or month, focus students' attention on one or more particularly important words. One week you might post and discuss the word "honesty." Following weeks might focus on friendship, trust, or perseverance.

Compliments

Facilitate a list of statements that help someone feel good. Create a master list of child-generated statements. Make this list into a wall poster.

Obviously, at primary level these compliments will be quite simple. Examples might include "I like your shoes," "I'd like to have lunch with you," "You're nice." This is your opportunity to expand the children's repertoire and their awareness.

Creative Esteem-Building

Try one or more of the following (adapted from Borba, 1988).

Ego booster plates: Students each have paper plates taped to their backs. All students are directed to write a compliment on each other student's plate.

Sparkle passes: Each day choose a student to receive a sparkle pass. The child takes this card with him throughout the day, and classmates write positive statements on it.

Positive pin: This is a pin with a positive statement on it, such as "I'm an optimist," "I like helping others," or "I'm friendly." Teachers and other adults at the school start off with the pins, which are handed to students as they exhibit the behavior. Each student with the pin, in turn, passes it on to the next deserving individual.

Yellow pages directory: Each student designs an ad—a yellow pages listing—to include the student's name and address, a description/advertisement of the student, and a phone number.

Acrostic Name Displays

Each student writes his or her name vertically, and then adds attributes horizontally. For example:

```
K  nowing
E  nergetic
N  ice
```

As a lead in, have a whole-class brainstorming of attributes beginning with different letters. Although this will feel playful to most students, in fact you are building their vocabulary as well as their self-awareness.

Writing extension: These can serve as the start of a writing project—students discover themselves by writing an essay, each major heading/paragraph being a theme derived from each attribute in order.

Affirmations and "I am" Statements

Have students write a positive statement—an affirmation—about themselves. Affirmations are positive, esteem-building statements. At intervals, perhaps three or four times throughout the day, the students silently remind themselves of their affirmation.

Students in small groups may take turns completing the statement "I am . . ." One student in the group is the recorder. The "I am" statement should reflect an activity or talent, for example, "I am a guitarist," "I am a photographer," "I am a swimmer." Younger students especially may tend to base their "I am" on something owned; help them to think instead in terms of what they do or like.

Team-building, self-awareness: These are good beginning of the year activities. They're also something to continue throughout the year.

Me Riddles and Mystery Person

On file cards, students create a "Who am I?" riddle by describing themselves without including their name. Classmates read each card, trying to guess the identity of the card. To increase learning and success, facilitate a list of characteristics and ideas to prompt student thinking. The list might include physical characteristics (e.g., hair color, length); family (e.g., number of siblings); interests, hobbies, and talents; and life experiences.

Language arts: Encourage students to focus on a more interesting, unique, or valued life experience, and then write about this one with more detail and depth.

Life science: You can do a trial run first with animal riddles/mysteries; this would be lower-risk for students who are hesitant to reveal themselves, or lack the self-awareness.

Social studies: Students choose their mystery country, or mystery president, etc.

■ FEEDBACK

You want to have a variety of tools for receiving feedback from students. Vary any of these depending upon your goals or the context.

Interest Surveys

These are very useful for gaining awareness of each student's interests, which are keys to motivating them. Early in the school year or course, an open-ended questionnaire/survey can be distributed to the students to fill out.

Questions on your survey might include the following:

- "What are your favorite hobbies, TV shows, activities?"
- "How do you feel about school? What are the best things you remember from last year? The worst things?"
- "Are grades important to you? To your parents? To your friends? What grades would you be content with in this course?"
- "Tell me about yourself, anything at all."

Elementary level: The benefits are great for the relatively minimal investment of time required. You can also conduct the survey more informally by talking one-to-one with each child, or when speaking to a parent.

Secondary level: Teachers with over 100 students each day may feel that they would never have the time to look over so many completed surveys. This is only partly true. One way to use the surveys is to quickly scan for overall interests, and then file them away. In the following weeks, periodically refer to the surveys of those students who are presenting problems with achievement, motivation, or discipline. A difficult or resistant learner can frequently be reached through his or her special interests.

Language arts, self-awareness: Cooperative learning groups can discuss the similarities and differences among their members, and write a summary or story related to the questionnaire.

Data collection and analysis: For a middle school social studies class, students can experience the design and data analysis that goes into creating an opinion poll.

Sticky-Note Feedback

At the end of the period or the day, students write a response to your question on a sticky note. They place the note on your door as they leave. For example: "What are the three things you learned today about writing essays?" "Did you have a nice day?" "What did you learn this week?"

Comments or Suggestions Box

Place a small box labeled "comments" in the room. A small square of paper can be distributed to each student, with directions as to what the students may write about. For example:

- "What was your favorite lesson last week?"
- "List one way that our class can be improved for learning."
- "Write a one-word description of your mood or feeling at this moment."

Students then anonymously place responses in the box.

You might choose to read these responses privately (safest option); selectively summarize and share them (more interesting option); or share them in full for the entire class (riskiest, but can be most trust-building).

Primary-level variation: Child draws faces—happy, undecided, sad.

Communication skills, life skills: Students learn to provide feedback in a positive and polite manner. Students will gradually develop more responsibility for their lives, and to exercise more choice in determining their future. If you share some of the comments, students will become more aware of the thoughts and feelings of all individuals, not just the comments of the most vocal. This is a good opportunity to hear the introspective students.

Reflection, self-awareness: These feedback/sharing opportunities can help students to reflect on their mood, on the lesson, or on numerous issues or concepts.

Social studies: Tallying the results enables the students to see how their comments compared with those of the group. For social studies, this can be a hands-on introduction to opinion polls, an omnipresent influence in our society—their construction, wording of questions, sources of sampling error.

Question box: A variation of the suggestion box, only now students submit questions. You may either assign a topic or leave it wide open. You don't even need the box. It's very simple—instead of having students answer a set of questions, assign them to ask questions regarding a reading assignment, film, science lab, or lesson.

Feedback Sheets

Students are handed an evaluation/reaction form, with questions such as these:

- "What was your favorite part of the week? Least favorite?"
- "What could you have done to make the week better for you?"
- "What could you have done to improve the week for someone else?"
- "What was your major accomplishment of the week?"
- "What types of classwork or assignments do you enjoy most? Least?"
- "List three things you learned this week that you will remember for one year."

Empower them even more . . .

As students get comfortable expressing themselves, have them create their own topic questions.

Evaluation by students: Give them opportunities to evaluate aspects of their world. Evaluation represents a natural culmination of any learning experience—one's growing mastery of the content provides the raw materials for analysis, synthesis, and ultimately evaluation. Here is a brief list of areas for evaluation.

Curriculum and instruction: Students can evaluate books, lessons, assignments, teaching methods. This does not need to be any formal or even scheduled process. You can merely sample student opinion casually by talking one-to-one with a variety of your students. (And please use your real voice, not your teacher voice.) You want the students to know that their feedback is valued. This leads to better feedback for you, which helps your teaching. And it leads to more thinking and ownership for the student. For both of you, it leads to a more authentic, trusting relationship. And it takes very little time.

Classroom climate: Students can provide feedback on such factors as lighting, spatial arrangement, bulletin boards, size of room, etc.

Thinking skills: Evaluate a TV show. "Is it realistic? Which actors are good? What do we mean by a good actor? What about the script, the photography, the plot?" Explore criteria for evaluating each of the above.

Language arts: Students evaluate a magazine of their choice.

Cooperative learning: Groups evaluate their performance according to specific criteria, e.g., sharing of ideas, contributions of all members, working together without friction.

Just Watching

There is such a wealth of feedback to be obtained from just noticing the children.

One method for maintaining your "watching notes" is to write them on self-stick mailing labels, with the observations of each student and the date on its own label.

Chapter 5
The Power of the Authentic

Here are a variety of tools and insights to extend children's thinking and learning beyond school, and beyond grades. Whenever possible, give students authentic reasons, purposes, content, and audiences to enhance learning and motivation.

■ YOUR AUTHENTIC VOICE

It's your show—be authentically you! You teach best when you let your personality shine through your teaching. It's your show—which is lots easier than putting on someone else's show. Mark Twain said, "If you tell the truth, you don't have to remember anything." When the real you does come through, your students perceive this. And it builds rapport. And trust. Because they like knowing they have a real person teaching them.

You have two voices—your real voice and your teacher voice. Your real voice is the more effective of the two. And with some of your students, and certainly your family and friends, your teacher voice is a serious liability. Your authentic voice also takes less effort, and leaves you with more energy at the end of the day.

Find your own voice and you become more effective. This does take trial and error. Yet once you connect with your real voice, your workload will be forever less. The following example illustrates your authentic voice in action.

Your Authentic Dilemmas

You face dilemmas in so many of your teaching decisions. For example, you may want to have high expectations for all your students, but you also want them to succeed. So how hard do you push them to excel? You may want students to have fun learning, but learning is not always fun—so what do you say when a student complains, "This isn't fun."

This is where the authentic dilemma comes in. Think aloud with students as you weigh each side of the dilemma. Let them know that it *is* a difficult decision you are making. Here are two authentic dilemmas you may want to share with students.

Higher expectations: Being accepting and pleasant *and* holding them accountable so they learn.

Late work: Wanting them to be successful *and* at the same time knowing that they need to get work done on time.

■ AUTHENTIC REASONS AND AUTHENTIC EXAMPLES

You will be far more persuasive with students when you give them authentic or real-world reasons and examples to explain *what you are doing and why*. This works with kindergartners through adults.

How will you know if your reason or example is authentic? It makes your rule, procedure, or explanation seem reasonable. It instantly makes sense to students. Students rarely argue with authentic reasons that are communicated with caring and integrity.

So if you have a rule for walking quietly down the halls, the reason for the rule should be authentic, i.e., it should make sense to the children because it is so reasonable and commonsense. One teacher shared with me how she was frustrated trying to get her kindergartners to walk single file. I asked her why she wanted them to walk single file. She could not give me (or her students) a plausible reason, other than that she wanted them to. It is very, very useful to have the reasons!

Authentic reasons do not just sell your case. They also provide a personalized and logical justification that fosters students' ownership and retention. Your classroom rules and procedures backed by authentic reasons are more likely to be followed, and more likely to be internalized and remembered.

Here is an example to justify higher academic expectations for 8th graders. "Right now your brain is able to learn more and faster, you have the time, and it's free. As you get older, your brain learns some things slower; you will have a job or family or be in college and have less time; and it will cost money to learn this. That is why I choose to be a teacher or coach who pushes you harder than you might push yourself. You might like me a little bit less now, because I have higher expectations, but you will thank me in 5 years."

What to do now: Take out some blank file cards and begin the process of writing down real-world reasons or examples to support your classroom rules, teaching methods, management philosophy, and curriculum. It will likely take some reflection to come up with reasons and examples that work well. Oftentimes, these will be your own stories. For example, to reinforce for students your strict rule on bullying, tell a story from your own life of when you were bullied. To reinforce your attitude of believing in the capabilities of your students, tell a story of a teacher who believed in you. When your stories are logical, entertaining, and personalized, you've done it!

■ AUTHENTIC AND STUDENT-CENTERED LEARNING

Authentic tasks are those that closely match what we actually do for a real purpose outside of school. Authentic does not have to be "useful." It only has to be pertinent to the real-world life of the student. If the student wonders why dinosaurs became extinct, an authentic task would be to find out the answer. The task is especially authentic when it has reason within the larger context beyond school, and students are engaged in it because it is something they own.

Similarly, authentic content includes the skills and concepts that are most pertinent in life beyond school. The power of authentic tasks is twofold:

> **1.** Students are doing it because they want to, and not because it is a class assignment or it is being graded. This leads to greater motivation and retention.
> **2.** Because the task correlates so well to the student's own experiences outside of school, the learning is much more likely to transfer to the student's life, and be applied throughout his or her life.

Here are two quick ways to make learning tasks more authentic.

Student-Generated Questions

Questions that emerge from the students themselves are more authentic and student-centered. I assigned 7th graders to pick any question that interested them, and to research the answer by using the phone. One of these 7th graders came in the next day excitedly sharing how he contacted the FBI to ask their opinion on capital punishment. This was *not* a student who reliably did his homework!

Incorporating Student Interests and Knowledge

Find out what interests students have. Connect the content to what they know. If a student enjoys fishing, do arithmetic with fishing. If a student loves music, have her write her essay on music. (This isn't rocket science.)

■ AUTHENTIC AUDIENCES

Create an audience for student work that extends beyond the teacher. This has an enormous effect on the level of effort and quality that students put into their work. This works even better if you sell students in an inspirational way on this audience. For example, "Kids, these projects will look so good when we post them in the hall. Be sure to check your spelling; we want the work to be amazingly good!"

Here are examples that progressively enlarge the audience from peers to school-wide to beyond the school:

> **1.** *Audience of a few peers:* Students have their work reviewed or assessed by one or more peers.
> **2.** *School-wide audience:* Student work is posted or shared within the classroom, on the wall outside the classroom, or on the wall outside the school office.
> **3.** *Audience of outside experts:* Student work is shared or presented to an audience that contains experts (writers, scientists, etc., from the community).
> **4.** *Audience beyond the school:* Student work is published in a class newsletter or a local community newspaper.

Authentic Letter-Writing

Think up writing tasks that have an audience beyond the teacher. What about a newspaper that the class produces and edits? Or student-authored books that are filed in the library with card catalog numbers?

Why have them write essays that nobody will ever read? Why practice writing letters that will never get sent? Therefore . . . have students write letters and emails to companies, to congressmen, to distant schools in other countries. Have them request information from a magazine ad.

Letters to Yourself

Have students write letters to themselves that they will open at the end of the year. Suggest possible topics for inclusion in their letters. This is an open-ended exercise for stimulating self-awareness.

In a more playful version, students design "time capsules," in which they write and draw, individually or in small groups, to describe their lives, interests, hopes, and goals. The capsules can be either sent home to parents or stored at school, and are opened at a specified future time.

VIP Letters

Each week designate a student as VIP. Classmates then write letters to that person. The VIP collects them and binds them into a book. You may have to help your children think of things to write about. Suggest that they share an interest, or ask the VIP questions.

Cooperation: You can arrange students in cooperative learning groups, where each team writes letters to the other teams.

Letter Exchanges

Write a friendly letter to your students early in the school year. You might write about your interests, family, or past experiences. Then throughout the year, as part of a journal-writing exercise, students are to write back to you. You can provide more structure by suggesting topics each week. Let students know that you don't have time to respond to each of their letters, but that you will respond in writing (one or two sentences) to their letters no less than, say, once per week. Any student who strongly desires a response can highlight, underline, or asterisk the part of their letter they want responded to.

Self-esteem, trust: These letters build rapport and self-esteem. Therefore, treat these letters as confidential, and do not assess their punctuation, grammar, or spelling.

■ INTERVIEWS

Your students can interview themselves or others, within the classroom and beyond the classroom. For creative writing, they can "invent" interviews with imaginary characters. And for social studies, they can create fictional interviews with historical characters.

Your objectives can be oriented to content or to such process skills as gathering information or communicating clearly.

Interviewing is an important life skill, with ready adaptations to most curricula. Start with the following examples, and then create your own.

Family Interviews: Students generate questions to ask their families. Students compile questions individually, or the entire class can collaborate to create a "question bank."

Data collecting and analysis: You or students design and carry out an opinion survey on an important current issue. Students can make phone calls to local experts, community resource people, and organizations—what a great way to gain practice with telephone skills.

Guest speakers: In addition to planning questions for the speakers, one or more self-reliant students can interview the speaker beforehand to arrange the details of the event—the topics, the scheduled time, location, and so forth.

Business interviews: Students collectively plan questions or information desired, then telephone, or visit in person, local businesses (e.g., travel agent, hardware store, utility company, library, hospital). Finally, learners share their interview notes with the class. Business interviews build students' awareness of the world, provide real-world communication and questioning practice, and reinforce that classroom learning does transfer beyond the classroom.

In-class interviews of students: A student volunteers to be interviewed by the class or by another student. Any interviewed student may say "pass" to any question. The interview can be designed around any content area or topic (e.g., world issues, chemicals in the environment, computers). Perhaps schedule an "interview of the week," whereby one student each week signs up to be interviewed for 10 minutes.

Chapter 6
The Enjoyment of Thinking

Thinking does take effort. If the task is enjoyable, students are more likely to make that effort. You will probably be familiar with many of these tools by one label or another. Again, most of these produce results far greater than the minimal preparation they require from you.

■ SOME BENEFITS OF DIVERGENT TASKS

Divergence exists in a situation or task where there is more than one right answer or approach. In contrast, convergent tasks have only a single correct answer. In the former a discussion produces many acceptable opinions and conclusions, while in the latter the teacher's job is to facilitate the students' converging on the same answer.

In life, divergent problems predominate. "Who should you marry?" "What should we do about global poverty?" "How much should the U.S. government spend to clean up pollution or to save an endangered species?" "Which of the stories that we read is the best?" These are divergent questions, where intelligent, informed discussion will rarely lead to the same answer for everyone.

In the classroom, our teaching often leads in the opposite direction, where we assess our kids on how well they can come up with the same answer that we have. There are important benefits to student learning and participation when tasks are divergent, with more than one right answer.

> 1. *Effort:* Divergent learning experiences encourage cooperation instead of competition, enthusiasm instead of apathy, empowerment instead of helplessness. If there is more than one answer, then more than one student can be correct. This encourages perseverance—students do not automatically stop thinking after the first answer is found. It also encourages tolerance and listening skills, because students learn that another student can have an answer that is both correct and different.
> 2. *Tolerance:* Divergent learning experiences nurture in us a willingness to respect the different beliefs of others. If you are accustomed to more than one right answer, then your curiosity (and not your contempt) will be aroused when you are exposed to other people's ideas.
> 3. *Participation:* More students participate in a discussion where there are several right answers. It's safer for them because they're less likely to be "wrong." Furthermore, it's more fun for kids when they don't have to be second-guessing the "one right answer" that the teacher is thinking.

Most of the tools in this section incorporate the benefits of these divergent tasks.

■ HYPOTHESIZE/ESTIMATE/PREDICT (HEP)

This is one of your core tools. It's simple, quick, versatile, and very effective. At the beginning of a lesson or task, ask your students to come up with a quick hypothesis, guess, estimate, or prediction related to a topic of study. There are at least four benefits of this tool:

> *Alertness and involvement:* The learner becomes more alert and more actively involved.
> *Tapping previous knowledge:* Students tap their previous knowledge and connect it with the present problem or topic.
> *Ownership:* Students take more ownership and responsibility for the subsequent task.
> *Thinking:* These skills of hypothesizing, estimating, and predicting are important life skills in their own right.

Hypotheses, estimates, and predictions are grouped together as one tool because of their similarities. In science, we generally call these "reasonable guesses" hypotheses. In math, the word "estimation" is prominent. And in social studies or literature, we often work with predicting or perhaps forecasting. In each case, our brain produces a preliminary answer that we then go on to verify by further inquiry, problem-solving, or analysis.

HEPs are exceedingly adaptable tools, as the following examples will illustrate.

Reading skills: Ask children to predict how long it will take them to read their particular book, or just a page in the book. Children often have inaccurate ideas of their reading skills, and you can help them here in better choosing the "just right" reading material. If it takes more than 3 minutes to read a page, the reading material is probably too difficult (Routman, 2003).

Lesson motivators, on-task behavior: "On a corner of your worksheet, write your prediction of how long it will take you to complete questions 1–10." Some children are rather unaware of just how much time they are off-task; this simple prediction can improve that awareness.

Social studies: "Take a guess how many Americans were killed in the Vietnam War? In World War II? In automobile accidents last year?"

Science: Keep a weather journal. Children can forecast tomorrow's weather.

Personal characteristics: Estimate the number in a year of . . . hamburgers you eat, miles you walk, hours slept, heart beats.

Group attributes, math: Estimate the percent (or fraction) of students in the class who . . . have more than two siblings, are over 4 feet tall, love pizza.

Measurements: Estimate first, then measure or research . . . the length of your desk in inches. The length of the room in meters. The volume of your bathtub in cubic feet. The cost of interstate highway per mile. The cost of a quart of milk in the year 2100 given an average inflationary rate of 5%.

Estimating time: At your signal, your students with eyes closed begin to estimate a minute. Each child raises his or her hand for a few seconds when he or she thinks 60 seconds are up. Record and graph the number of hands up for each time interval. The result is a more-or-less bell-shaped graph. Have students predict how the shape of the graph will change if the activity is repeated.

Topic/reading predictions: Students are given a topic or reading selection, and list words they think will be included in that topic or reading.

True/false predictions: Students are given a list of statements related to a topic, and predict for each one whether it is true or false. After the reading or lecture or activity, students go back and see which of their true/false predictions was correct.

Estimating and Measuring Games

Estimate, then measure: Play a game where students must estimate first, before they measure. Items might include . . . dimensions of items in the room, such as desks, pencils, floor length, or volumes, such as liquid in variously shaped containers. You can estimate and measure heights of buildings or trees—on a sunny day measure the height and shadow length of a known object (e.g., a yardstick held vertically), and measure the shadow length of the tree or building. It's a simple ratio problem—ask a math person if you're stumped!

Accuracy throws: With a ball, students aim for a spot against a wall. They record the distance between their throw and the target. They can average a number of throws. They can estimate their accuracy first, then subtract the difference between their estimate and their actual result. You can practice metric measurements through play.

Volume game: Start with a container partly filled with water, and several empty containers of various shapes. Students predict the level to which the water will rise when poured into each of the other containers. The child who guesses closest roles a die to determine how many points are received. The person with the most points after 5 rounds, or 15 minutes, wins.

Variations: Students can practice this game by themselves, or at home with parents. If the water is poured into a measuring cup, students will become more familiar with units of volume. Or have students make their own measuring cup, by marking units on a plastic cup, based upon known volumes poured from an existing measuring cup.

Non-standard units: Students measure objects using as units one or more of the following: toothpicks, hand width, shoe length, width of notebook paper.

Odd entities: Estimate and measure the dimensions of various objects in the room—arm lengths, thumb widths, length of longest hair, shortest pencil in the room. Of course, you can also measure the usual . . . desks, length of room, or students' heights.

Higher-level math: Estimate surface areas or volumes of desks, floor, wall, and books. Determine ratios and relationships of arm length to height, waist measurement to height, head circumference to arm length. Have students creatively explore other measurements and relationships, and compare students' ratios. Estimate, then measure, volumes by displacement of rocks, clay, fruits. Measure the ratio of jar lid circumferences to diameters; of course, you end up with pi, approximately 3.14.

Reading: Measure your reading speed for several styles of writing, such as easy fiction, the sports page of the newspaper, or a section in the encyclopedia.

■ PROCESS SHARING

When the answer isn't the most important thing, teach for the process. Two related tools accomplish this—process sharing and thinking aloud.

Even where there is one right answer, there is always more than one right way to get there. You and students can think aloud as together you explore a problem. This fosters students' metacognition—the process of being aware of and directing one's own thinking.

Research is showing that experts process their observations and thinking differently than novices. When you think aloud, your students—the novices—learn from your modeling how to become more expert. Instead of asking students for the answer, ask your students the following questions.

"What did you do to solve the problem? What did you try first? Did it work? Did you have to try other ways? Did you get stuck? What did you do when you got stuck?"

After one or more students share their problem-solving approach, ask others: "Did anyone else try a different way?" "Which way did you like the most?" "What would you have done similarly or differently to solve that problem?"

Process sharing is quite enjoyable to most students. It enables kids to share with pride their own strategies. And it is the child's own strategies that have the most value to the child—these build upon, and connect to, what the child already knows. Thus, these will be retained.

Additionally, students are quite interested in seeing how their own thinking strategies compare to those of their peers—especially where there isn't a single correct answer. So you'll have good class participation with process sharing.

■ THINKING ALOUD

Thinking aloud comes in two versions.

The first version is when you think aloud so students can observe and learn from your thinking. When you are modeling a new skill, or solving a problem, think aloud with the students so they can see what strategies you are using. Otherwise, students can see the result of your thinking—the answer or the performance—but the actual thinking remains hidden from view.

The second version is when students are asked to think aloud as they solve a problem or practice a skill. This thinking aloud can be done with whole group instruction, or in smaller cooperative learning groups. When learners think aloud, you are better able to assess what strategies your students are using, and if particular students need further assistance in choosing or using appropriate strategies.

Reading: Thinking aloud is excellent for reading instruction. Periodically, you can pause when you are reading to the class, and model the use of any one or more decoding or comprehension strategies. For example . . .

"Huh, I'm not sure what they mean here. That's a word I don't know. Maybe I can figure out what it means from the rest of the sentence . . ."

"Wow, I wasn't paying enough attention to what I was reading. I'm going to reread that paragraph . . ."

■ RESPONSE REPERTOIRES

Every day in the classroom, you interact with your students. You respond to their behaviors, their comments, and their questions. To keep them alert, expand your repertoire of responses. You'll stimulate more thinking, or at least wake them up. Try the following.

Neither agree nor disagree: Try to not always agree or disagree with students. Agreement and disagreement tends to inhibit further thinking by students.

Ask for reasons or elaboration or examples: Instead, ask students to explain their thoughts, to give reasons for their opinions, to extend thoughts or create new ideas.

Ask who else agrees or disagrees: This motivates students to continue thinking about the question or task being discussed.

Raise a new idea: Based upon student responses, lead the discussion to other insights.

Neutral gestures: Respond with gestures or comments that indicate your interest or acknowledgment, but not necessarily agreement. For example: "O.K.," or by a nod of the head, a smile, or holding up one finger after another as each student responds in turn.

I wonder. . . : There are times we ask students just too many questions. Try the "I wonder" strategy, a user-friendly alternative: "I wonder how your story will end" instead of "How does your story end?"

■ WAIT TIME

When you provide students with more time to respond to a question, the quality and quantity of student responses is improved. Furthermore, the quieter and more reflective students will participate more. Listen patiently and actively.

Wait while students ponder their thoughts. It is not necessary for you to rush in with expertise and corrections at each turn of the discussion.

A wait time of approximately 5–8 seconds, though it can feel initially like an unbearably long silence, will eventually grow comfortable and effective.

"After I ask the question, I am going to wait while all of you think. So don't put your hands up till I tell you I'm ready."

■ CREATIVE THINKING MODES

We are able to think better when we develop the ability to consciously shift gears into different modes of thinking, according to the needs of the moment. So, for example, we might decide in one situation to shift into a logical-rational mode, or to an emotional-feeling mode, or a creative mode.

Why not let students become more aware of their own modes? Label and model them, starting perhaps with the creative mode. This metacognitive skill of gear-shifting is a significant quality of proficient thinkers.

"O.K., those are all good answers, now switch to creative mode, and come up with an additional five reasons." In creative mode, you are tolerant, even encouraging, of those far-fetched ideas that your logical-rational mode or your critical mode would reject.

"O.K., now switch back to critical mode, and judge which of your answers is the best." By explicitly directing students to a particular mode, the students do not have to second-guess when you want creativity and when you don't. You certainly don't want students in creative mode when they're filling in the little circles on a standardized test!

Seven Benefits of Creative Mode

- Can re-engage students at the start, middle, or end of a lesson
- Stimulates higher-level thinking
- Can lead-in to creative writing
- Provides opportunity for each student's individuality to be expressed
- Adds some novelty, or changes the pace or the routine
- Yields extra smiles or laughs to brighten up our day
- Provides enormously practical experience for coping with real-world challenges, the most important of which are open-ended

■ GRAPHIC ORGANIZERS AND CONCEPT MAPPING

Graphic organizers are a simple and powerful way to visually structure information and ideas. You can visually organize virtually anything: comparison/contrast, time lines, flow charts for a science experiment, cycles in nature, outlines for essays, project management. One of the benefits of these graphic organizers is that children are generally more motivated when the learning is visual—and especially if they get to use color.

Assess student knowledge prior to teaching a social studies unit: A concept or picture is drawn in the middle of a blank piece of paper. Working rapidly—a time limit of 3–5 minutes can be imposed—students generate related concepts branching out from the starter concept. Glance at their work, and in very little time you know how you will need to design instruction for that unit. Briefly jot notes of where you see unexpected misconceptions or gaps in student knowledge.

Consequence Map

One of my favorite types of concept maps is what I refer to as a "consequence map"—which follows cause/effect or interrelationships from any starting point.

That starting point can be the actions of a character in a novel, a change in school policy, global warming, the invention of electricity. These are similar in form to mind maps, or concept maps. The initial starting point is written in the middle of the paper. Consequences, whether probable or improbable, are recorded radiating outward like spokes from a wheel. Of course, each of those consequences or effects then leads to others, which also lead to others, producing one or more "consequence chains." These chains help students see that everything is interconnected—there are always unanticipated side effects of any action or situation, and predicting the future is extraordinarily difficult for these reasons.

Both maps and chains can be accomplished in one assignment. Try these as lead-ins to a social studies or science lesson. Combine them with scenarios.

Writing, outlining, main ideas, etc: Have students do a consequence brainstorm, and then create an outline from it. Students have no trouble creating an essay from their consequence brainstorms, because these already have a sequential (i.e., cause/effect) structure to follow.

The brainstorming of consequences from personal actions (e.g., choosing to finish high school) leads into self-awareness, goal-setting, and classroom discussion.

■ Focus Shifts

Focus shifting is the intentional redirecting of your thoughts or senses in another direction. Too often, our habits direct our attention, and the breadth of our perceptions becomes ever narrower. We notice what we noticed yesterday. Each day, we look at the world through the same lens.

Remember to frequently shift your focus. Shift from near to far, to the shapes of buildings, or the colors in the sky. If you tend to notice colors, shift your focus to shapes. If you tend to notice tastes of foods, focus instead on textures. Remember to continually rekindle your sense of appreciation and wonder.

Focus shifting is an outstanding way to jolt your brain. It's one way to keep life interesting and enjoyable. And it's extremely crucial as a career and life skill for maintaining awareness of one's global environment.

What to Do Now

Incorporate focus-shifts directly into lesson plans: Whatever the assignment, students can be directed to shift focus between the following:

- Self and surroundings
- Details and overview
- Classroom and real world
- Head and heart

Obviously, you wouldn't bombard students with all of the above shifts in any one lesson. Whatever your teaching style, a few focus shifts will give students fresh perspectives, and probably more neuron connections in their brains to reinforce their learning.

Social studies: Shift from the student's own point of view to the likely viewpoint of others.

Math: Shift the focus from the answer to the process.

Information literacy: In any subject where enormous quantities of information are taught, a shift from knowledge to feelings can prevent students from suffering severe cases of cognitive overload.

Spelling and spatial processing: As a mnemonic, you might encourage students occasionally to observe the outlined shapes of spelling words. Students can outline the shape with line or yarn.

Art: One technique that helps artists to "see" is observing the space between the objects—negative space—rather than the shapes of the objects themselves.

■ SYSTEMS DESIGN

Systems design includes a broad range of open-ended synthesis projects. This is one of my favorite tools. It has all the ingredients I love—a motivating and challenging experience, choice, a variety of learning modes, student success, and, best of all, it takes very little teacher effort.

All students—from slow learners to gifted, analytical to artistic, shy to social—can succeed. You have many choices of systems to design:

- Imaginary or ideal island
- Political system
- Civilization on another planet
- Ideal house or playground
- A best friend
- School menu
- Birthday party
- An economic system
- Any authentic project
- Service learning project

Systems design facilitates reinforcement and synthesis of content as well as right/left brain creativity. It is readily amenable to performance assessment, and fosters cooperative learning and student sharing. It validates the range of individual learning styles and multiple intelligences, and builds self-awareness and self-esteem. Whew!

You may choose specific elements that children are directed to incorporate into their systems. For example, an island design for an earth science class might emphasize landforms, natural resources, and climate. On the other hand, an island design for social studies might emphasize such features as population size, transportation, and political systems.

To stimulate such life skills as discussion, cooperation, decision-making, and leadership, consider establishing students in groups, with members reaching agreement on their creation.

Middle school social studies: "Working in groups of three, design an ideal country. Incorporate each of the following elements: political environment (i.e., government), economy (i.e., sources of revenue, types of industry), the people (i.e., values and attitudes, lifestyle, leisure activities), physical and biological environment (i.e., land use, population density, plant and animal life, treatment and recycling of wastes), significant issues and how they are being resolved. Projects are to be a combination of the following: written descriptions; creative writing; maps, models and other visuals; tables showing data and analyses."

Synthesis, projects, and closure: Systems design is one of the best project types for the end of a course or unit. Not so obvious is that the same project assigned at the start of a course will enable students to readily compare their pre- and post-learning.

Games Design

Provide each group or team with one or more balls, hula hoops, or other objects. The objective is for the group to design a game that uses all of the specified equipment, and actively involves the players. Give the class a time limit, for example 10 minutes.

Language arts, communication skills: Each team writes up a rules manual for their game, including graphics, or teaches their game to other groups.

Problem-solving: Children anticipate potential problems with their game and brainstorm ways to improve it.

Creative thinking: Groups generate creative variations of their game.

Design Technology

In this category are the opportunities for students to work with materials to construct a functional product. Some students will be extremely careful with their planning, some will dive right in, but all students should be provided with these types of exciting, playful, hands-on experiences.

Here are some familiar examples that teachers have used for years.

▸ *Paper Airplane Contest*

Let students generate the rules and procedures. This includes paper size and type, use of other materials, number of trials, indoors or out, and assessment such as accuracy, total distance, or duration of flight.

Decision-making, teamwork, thinking skills: In addition to motivation value, students learn to think and plan logically, cooperatively, and fairly.

Science process skills: Reinforce skills and concepts such as variables, hypotheses, experimental design, and data collection and analysis.

- **Build Bird Nests**

  Primary level: First, bring in a sample unused nest. Let the children examine it. Then, with materials such as grass, twigs, mud, students each construct a nest of their own. As a result of this experience, it is quite easy to lead into reading or writing more about birds.

- **Bridge Design**

  Using a specified quantity of newspaper, students design the strongest bridge of a specified length capable of supporting weight from the center without buckling. Similar learning outcomes as for paper airplane contest.

- **Egg Drop**

  Using materials such as a Styrofoam cup, a sheet of paper, and masking tape, students build an egg carrier that will prevent a raw egg from breaking when dropped from a predetermined height.

- **Creative Design**

  Using materials of your choosing, students design a butterfly, a fish, a model of a house. Experiment with the following: dough, pipe cleaners, Popsicle sticks, paper, spaghetti.

■ DISCREPANT EVENTS

A discrepant event is any experience that produces a result contrary to what you would expect. Discrepant events are surprising, engaging, thought provoking. They stimulate students' curiosity, and drive learners to inquire and to investigate further. Science teachers are a rich source of discrepant events, and many of them are very quick attention-getters.

Each of these is a prime source for inquiry or further experimentation. Each of these discrepant events is a source of enjoyment for children. They are a means to reach a child who speaks a different language, a way to spark smiles and laughter from a child whose parents are getting divorced, a way to build rapport with a difficult student.

In each example given, the intent is to get the most student learning and engagement from the least amount of teacher effort or time.

Here are a few of my favorites. There are many, many others.

Cotton Balls in Water

Fill a clear glass or plastic cup to within a millimeter or two of the rim. Now ask the kids to predict how many cotton balls will fit in the glass before the water overflows. They will probably say five or six. As it turns out, cotton balls are almost entirely empty space filled with air, so you will see ten or twenty or more go into the glass, with the level of the water barely rising at all.

Math problem-solving: What percent of the cotton ball is just air? What is the cost per pound of cotton balls?

Physical science: Cotton balls are almost entirely empty space, and are a model for the structure of atoms and molecules, which are also mainly empty space. Likewise, the cotton balls also represent clouds, which from a distance appear solid.

The Coat Hanger Chime

Cut and shape a cheap metal coat hanger into a "U" shape. Attach cotton twine to the middle of the U so you have two free ends of approximately 12 or 15 inches each. Now hold each of the string ends to the middle of each ear, with the metal dangling below. Let the metal swing gently into any object (e.g., a desk), and it makes the most surprising and pleasant chiming noise.

Science: Experiment with different variables to see which ones influence the sound. You can change the shape and length of the coat hanger, change the type or length of the string, or change the object you strike against. This is a very simple science experiment that reinforces process skills of hypothesizing, experimental design, testing variables, etc.

Burn a Macadamia Nut

Take a single macadamia nut and pierce it with a long pin or a straightened paper clip. Holding the end of the paper clip, position the nut above a lit wooden match or candle flame. It will take a few seconds for the nut to ignite. The amazing part is that a substantial flame will continue for 5 full minutes! What an experience of the calories in a nut!

Nutrition, calories: Quick lead-in to foods and calories.

Water Drops on a Penny

Using eyedroppers, students place drops of water, one at a time, onto a penny. The goal is to get the most drops onto the coin before the water flows off the edge. Due to the surface tension of water, a rather large dome of water will form, surprising and thrilling the students. I have seen kids from kindergarten through middle school really enjoy this friendly competition to get the most drops on the penny.

Fine motor skills, counting, data collection: This is an excellent activity for young ones.

Math, graphing, surface area, interpolation: Measure the number of drops that can be placed on a dime, penny, and quarter. Graph the data—number of drops on the Y-axis, surface area of the coin in square mm on the X-axis. By interpolation, predict the number of drops that a nickel could hold.

The important idea: Please . . . what is important is *not* whether you ever figure out how to do the interpolation part of the previous activity! The crucial point is this: *You can teach grand, sophisticated, and engaging skills and concepts using the barest minimum of simple materials, with minimal prep, and no worksheets to photocopy.* Tap your wisdom, your creativity, and your energy, and you shall set yourself free.

■ SCIENTIFIC THINKING: SYSTEMS AND PARTS OF THE SYSTEM

The following hands-on activities illustrate simple, generic ways that you can enhance students' thinking and science skills. Each one illustrates the enormous power that comes from understanding variables and parts of a system. The ability to see the whole as well as the parts is one of the most significant goals of science education. And it transfers beautifully to virtually any discipline.

Example #1: Balloons and Static Electricity

Rub an inflated balloon on your hair or a fabric, and of course the static charge will allow it to stick to a wall. But, there's more. There are actually quite a number of variables that influence the strength of this static cling. And students can readily experiment with these variables. Here are the variables:

> Balloon: shape, size, color, amount inflated
> Rubbing: amount of time, type of material, direction, which surface of balloon was rubbed.
> Wall: type of material (e.g., window, wall, whiteboard), roughness
> Environment: air pressure, humidity, air currents, temperature

The generic essentials for getting the most from scientific experimentation is to create the most student engagement and inquiry from the least amount of teacher prep time and consumable or messy materials. Thus, in this case, all you need is a balloon, and yet all the ingredients for scientific inquiry are present: hypotheses, variables, data collection, discussion, conclusions.

Generally I will have student teams each choose one variable at a time to investigate, such as round balloons versus elongated balloons. And we decide on a way to measure the strength of the static charge. One way to quantify the charge is to successively tape one small paper clip at a time to the side of the balloon as it is sticking to the wall. Eventually, the weight of two or seven paper clips pulls the balloon down.

Example #2: Plant Germination and Growth

As with the balloons and static electricity experiment, there are a number of variables influencing a seed or plant:

> Light: amount, type (daylight, fluorescent, incandescent), or lack of light
> Water: amount, fresh water vs. salty water, etc.
> Seed or plant: type of plant
> Soil: sandy, clay, loam, etc.

Each student or team can pick one question to test. For example, "Does a seed need light to germinate?"

After investigating plants, you can create a friendly competition with bean seeds. Students are in charge of each of the variables above (water, light, soil, etc.), and the competition is to have the seed germinate and grow to 12 inches in the shortest amount of time. Students maintain a log describing what they did.

Example #3: Social Studies

Brainstorm with children everything that makes up a city or country or government. Each of these parts of the system can then be explored in more depth or made into a concept map. Or you and students can take the list of those parts and have students then design their own city or country or government—each design addressing all of the various parts. This last exercise is an example of a "system design" tool.

Scientific Thinking: Inquiry and Experimental Design

You don't need materials or time to have students doing science. You just need to suggest engaging ideas, and at least some of the kids will carry them out. They just need a bit of prompting from you.

"Is yawning contagious with dogs?" Here is a simple experiment: Watch your dog closely for 15 minutes, and count the number of yawns. Then yawn repeatedly in front of your dog for another 15 minutes and count the yawns again. Did your yawning seem to influence your dog's yawning?

"What's the best bait to use to catch fruit flies?" Put a variety of different baits into your fruit fly traps. Be sure you have lots of fruit flies around. Wait a day or two. Whichever bait caught the most fruit flies wins.

"What's the smallest amount of salt you can put into a quart of water and still be able to taste it?"

"Can slugs hear? Can they see? Do they remember where they live?"

Surveys and Data Collection

Design a survey to collect and analyze information, such as preferences (e.g., Pepsi vs. Coke; hot dogs, burgers, neither). Design with students an appropriate data collection form. From the collected data, test one or more hypotheses. For example, test the hypothesis that your 8th graders prefer a different salad dressing than the 6th graders. Primary students can collect data on the most popular car color in the parking lot—my students really enjoyed doing this, especially the student whose turn it was to have the clipboard!

Chapter 7
The Joy of Language and Communication

I have collected here a wide variety of tools to stimulate the many different parts of the brain, and the many different types of learners. Experiment. Enjoy.

■ COMMUNICATION PRECISION TOOLS

Give your students some nonthreatening and open-ended opportunities to practice communicating clearly and more precisely. The ability to communicate effectively is one of those vital skills we can teach our kids.

But how do you provide this practice without resorting to the tedium of endless drills, worksheets, warnings, frowns, bribes, and stickers? Through nonthreatening, highly participatory and playful tasks, and a variety of experiences, e.g., auditory, visual, tactile, musical, and written.

There are many variations in modality that are possible with this tool.

Written: Students write directions for making a peanut butter and jelly sandwich or how to eat an Oreo cookie or how to give map directions from school to their home. Be sure to transfer and connect these concrete, playful experiences to your other lessons involving clear communication. If *you* don't make the connections clear, you can be sure most students won't either.

Spatial: Students draw diagrams showing an arrangement of pattern blocks or other objects, and a partner arranges the objects according to the diagram.

Graphic: Students create accurate drawings of leaves so that a partner can match a particular drawing to the correct leaf.

Musical, rhythmic: Students describe a piece of music, or a sequence of notes, so that a partner can match the description to the piece.

The following examples offer different structures for the Communication Precision Technique.

Communication Precision Partners

Students sit in pairs, with their backs together. Student A of the pair has a drawing or arrangement of objects, which must be communicated to student B, who must duplicate student A's pattern. Student B may not talk or ask for any clarification. This activity can be done most concretely with the arrangement of objects on a desk. The teacher can provide handouts of designs to be communicated, or students can draw/arrange as they choose.

This is a highly motivating, active, whole-brain method for teaching the importance of communicating clearly and accurately. It involves spatial and sequencing skills, following directions, and reviewing shapes and positions. It can be done on graph paper to reinforce coordinates and graphing, or using pattern blocks in primary grades. You can make the activity easier by letting student B ask questions, or letting student A observe student B while giving the directions.

"How-to" Writing

A teacher in one of my workshops had her students delight in choosing something to teach their classmates. They each wrote a how-to paper—how to start a snowmobile, do skateboard tricks, clean a rat's cage, make cookies.

Message Chains

These familiar games require that a message be conveyed accurately from one individual to the next through a chain of several or more students. The message may be almost anything: a sentence, a story, a musical rhythm, or a tactile "drawing" on one's back.

In the "gossip game," or "telephone," a message is told to one student, who whispers the message to a second student in line, who whispers it to a third, and so on. The last student in line shares the message out loud.

▸ Sentence Chains

Here is a variation to encourage students to use more descriptive language. Start with students in groups of four or five. The first person in each group starts with a very simple sentence, e.g., "The dog ran." The second student adds one word to the sentence, e.g., "The large dog ran." Each student in turn within the group adds a word. Finally, the groups compare their final sentences.

Music: Have the kids practice a variety of rhythms from different types of music. Help your students learn to improve their retention of these rhythms.

▸ Back Drawings

Students form into two or more parallel lines of approximately 5–10 individuals per line, with all students facing in the same direction. The students at the rear in each line are shown a simple line pattern to duplicate by writing with their finger on the back of the person in front of them. Each person in the line in turn interprets what was drawn on their back, and then to the best of their ability, writes that same design on the back of the person in front of them. When the drawing reaches the first person in line, that person draws the pattern on the chalkboard. Finally, the original drawing and the final interpretations are held up for the class to compare. The wide range of final drawings is enormously entertaining!

Cooperation and team building: This game is worthwhile purely for the joy of it, and for the team spirit that prevails.

Foreign language: As a metaphor, back drawings beautifully demonstrate the development of numerous languages from a single source. In this case, the separate lines represent peoples who became geographically isolated from each other, with the result that unique dialects and even languages evolve over the succeeding generations.

Language, primary level: Use back drawings as a playful way for students to practice their letters or spelling words. Children's brains must visualize what is felt but not seen, thus stimulating learning through a combination of sensory modalities.

Social studies, research reports, critical thinking: Here's a concrete experience illustrating the importance of getting firsthand information. Connect this "play" to the writing of research reports, critically assessing news reports, or judging the inaccuracy of rumors.

Rumors: This activity shows how unreliable information can be when it is circulated from one person to another.

Biology: A good example to illustrate is how populations of a species when separated geographically will diverge in their traits.

■ An Enjoyment of Words

Words can be immensely satisfying when they connect meaningfully with our lives. And they can be satisfying when they create laughter—do not overlook this entertainment value of words.

Acronyms

Make the familiar strange; make the strange familiar. Invent humorous and frivolous acronyms. "It's an NSD" (nice sunny day). "We have an NPS" (noisy pencil sharpener). Acronyms are one way to create a shared culture that helps build community. It is analogous to sports fans rallying behind the same home team.

Picture Charades

One person draws a picture to represent a word, while the other team members or class members must guess the word being drawn. Give the team a specific time limit for guessing, e.g., 2 minutes. This game is enjoyable as well as creative; minimal artistic ability is required.

Middle school science content: You can take a few minutes to draw pictures of science terms from this unit, e.g., bacteria, igneous rock, molecule.

Validating student talents: Appoint an artistic student in your class to be the illustrator.

Word Banks, Word Collections

Create a collection of words on any topic. When sorted and read aloud as a poem, these collections can be quite enjoyable. Here's a word collection of textures:

> Slippery, prickly, satiny and smooth,
> Slimy and soft, slivery and rough,
> Sharp and dull, hot and cold.

Vocabulary: This is a version called "word explosions." Students are given a single word (e.g., heart), and are to find (from recall or from a dictionary) compound words and phrases containing the word (e.g., heartbreak, open heart surgery, etc.)

Question/Answer Plays

These are for creativity—creative writing, creative thinking, and fun. One student of a pair writes a question, the teacher specifying either a who, what, or where type. The other partner writes an answer of the same type, without knowing what the question will be. Questions are then randomly paired with answers. The result is sometimes meaningless, sometimes dull, and sometimes hilariously funny. For example . . .

"Where" questions: "Where do they put the people who pull off the little tags on mattresses that say 'It is illegal to remove this tag'?"

Some "Where" answers: "Inside the toaster," "New York City."

"Who" questions: "Who sings to themselves on a crowded bus with people listening?" "Who eats hamburgers without ketchup?"

Some "who" answers: "Abraham Lincoln," "A person looking for a dog," "My pet goldfish," "The president of the United States."

"What" questions: "What happened when the thirty invisible extraterrestrials walked off unseen with 150 burgers in Toledo, Ohio?"

"What" answer: "There was an earthquake."

Creative Labels and Mnemonics

Add spark to an assignment—students invent creative labels for their work. The labels can be titles, acronyms, maxims, aphorisms, adages, subtitles, and analogies. Even simple, everyday worksheets can be spiced up with clever titles:

> "The Five Greatest Math Problems in the Known Universe"
> "Revenge of the Pronouns"
> "Spelling Words for Fun and Profit"

If something already has a title, subtitles can be very entertaining diversions. For example:

> "Charlotte's Web: A Family Story for the Spider in All of Us"
> "American History: 557 Pages and It's All Small Print"

Learning and Retention: As a mnemonic—a memory tool—students create or learn acronyms.

> The acronym "Roy G Biv" has been in use for eons (at least since I took earth science in 9th grade). It stands for red-orange-yellow-green-blue-indigo-violet. These are the colors of the spectrum in order.
> "A meter's over 3 foot 3; it's longer than a yard you see."

Spelling: HERE and tHERE. A PIEce of PIE. You hEAR with your EAR.

Positive classroom environment: Do you have kids that are good at complaining, but need a little help suggesting something better? Try responding with "That's just 'posaltific'!" (terrific positive alternative) when a student politely and positively shares suggestions instead of sharing complaints.

Alliteration

When two or more words in sequence begin with the same sound, this alliteration is pleasing to the ear. Encourage students to come up with alliterative titles to their essays or stories, to use alliteration in some of their writings, and to find alliteration in their daily experiences, such as in advertising.

Whole language: Children love the playful repetition of sounds.

Creative writing: Suggest to your students that they include alliteration in their titles.

Literature, consumer awareness, advertisements: Draw your students' attention to the widespread use of alliteration all around them. Keep a list of as many examples as they can find in advertising as well as literature.

Playful Repetitions

Take any recently learned information (e.g., "George Washington was the first U.S. president") and have students repeat the information using different voices and facial expressions. Students whisper it, ask it, try different accents and pitches, laugh it, and cry it.

Retention: Use this to both break up the routine and to foster better retention through the repetitions. It's usually for *occasional* use, not every day.

Fictional Report Cards

Students make up report card comments or a letter to a parent for any characters—real or fictional—studied or read about in class. For example, your 5th graders will pretend to be Abraham Lincoln's 5th grade teacher, writing a letter to Abe's mom. Encourage humor.

■ Playful Storytelling

Storytelling has marvelous potential for learning and enjoyment. A story ignites the visual imagery of the brain, thus grabbing students' attention and holding it.

Your own storytelling: You will certainly want to transform some of your lectures into stories—add facial expression, vary your voice, throw in some good timing and gestures, and toss in some movement. Enjoy yourself.

Depending upon your choice of story and the focus, your objectives can be oriented toward a wide range of skills or outcomes: speaking skills, listening, learning and retention of concepts, creativity, sharing and positive classroom environment, self-esteem.

Try the following variations to motivate your students' enjoyment of their own stories.

Three Truths

This is a playful tool with diverse applications. Each student thinks of four brief anecdotes or statements to be shared in small groups. Three of the statements should be true and one false. The four statements are shared with the group, with each of the listeners guessing which statement is false.

"Three Truths" is quite motivational for any age, including adults. You may want to model the activity first—students love discovering facts about their teacher. This is an excellent beginning-of-year icebreaker or a good rapport-builder at any time.

Writing: Each of the truths, separately or in combination, can serve as the starting point for a writing assignment. Encourage students to elaborate on the truth, adding details and connections. Or encourage them to create a story from their nontruth.

Speaking skills and storytelling: The oral sharing of the three truths is a nonthreatening starting point for breaking down the fear of presenting to a group. Students who are comfortable sharing with the small groups may volunteer to share for the whole class. Encourage speakers to give convincing details and a lively presentation.

Practice and review: Have students write up three true statements and one false for topics they are studying. This clever packaging of what are essentially multiple-choice questions is a motivating review before a test.

Outrageous Truths List

Staff team building and enjoyment: Put a blank sheet of paper in the staff room, titled "Outrageous Truths." Whenever teachers are in the staff room, they are invited to add any interesting or bizarre truths from their own lives. Nobody signs their contribution, and the list continues to grow each week, with teachers obviously intrigued as to who owns each contribution. Finally, set aside a few minutes at a staff meeting to divulge names.

Whose Story Is It?

Three or four students form a group to privately share and choose a true story that happened to one of them. Then each student in turn presents to the class a brief narrative of that story as if it were his or her own. The class guesses, by a show of hands, which of the children was actually telling the truth.

Public speaking, drama: Students become more confident speaking in front of the class. They develop their storytelling ability and their communication skills in general.

Listening skills, critical thinking: For the audience, this activity stimulates active listening and critical thinking. Students must grapple with subtle, often right-mode, clues as to the reliability of each story version. This is a good lead-in to propaganda—how do we tell truth from falsehood?

Collaborative Storytelling

This is a collaborative effort adapted from *Playfair* by Matt Weinstein and Joel Goodman. You begin the story, either true or fictional. At any time, a student may interrupt by saying, "I was there," to which the leader replies, "And what did you see my friend?" The student then adds his or her details, being sure not to refute what anyone has previously said. After describing what he or she saw, the group exclaims "Aha!" The teacher continues where the story left off, until another student calls out "I was there."

Listening skills: This tool motivates listening skills, creativity, cooperation, and a few good laughs. One extension is to relive an actual event in history using this activity.

Social studies: Students in groups prepare their stories in advance, with each student choosing parts of the history to retell as a first-person account.

Storytelling Grid

Students and teacher each divide a sheet of paper into a grid of four to eight boxes. Within each box, a little sketch or symbol is drawn to represent a particular story, anecdote, or event related to that author's life. Students may volunteer to stand up and share a story represented by one of their boxes. You can have a specified time during the week for this sharing.

Let the class choose the box that the student or teacher is to share—the act of choosing encourages the students to be more attentive to the story and to participate more fully as active listeners.

Outrageous Story Math

Students create word problems for math that are innovative, crazy, creative. You can leave the task wide open, or you can set up a structure for the problems:

> "Each of your stories must contain a division problem."
> "Your story should contain the multiplication of 8 × 3."

Gifted/talented: Assign a student or two to create an entire worksheet of these creative stories, along with an answer sheet showing any problem-solving steps.

■ Quotations

I am an optimist. It does not seem too much use being anything else.
Winston Churchill

Quotations are simple, versatile, and effective. They readily facilitate students' higher levels of thinking and feeling. Furthermore, when students collect the quotations themselves, they take greater ownership for their learning. Applications to your classroom are many.

Motivation, student ownership: Have students find their favorite quotes from readings, newspapers, or TV. Share them orally or in writing to encourage your class to reflect more deeply about what they are reading.

Language: Use quotations to ignite in students an awareness of the poetry in language.

Positive classroom climate: Share students' finds, thus helping you and your kids become more aware of their own and other students' values, interests, and individuality.

Positive attitudes, leadership, and historical figures: You and students collect quotes, such as the previous quote from Winston Churchill.

School spirit: Best quotes can be included in the school bulletins, or posted prominently in or near the school office.

Art: Write quotes up poster size, using creative lettering, calligraphy, colors, or computers. Post the quotations on a wall, door, or bulletin board. Try the outside of your door, for visitors and students to notice; change the quote each couple of weeks.

Writing: Present a quotation to the class and have each student write/discuss what that quote means to her or him.

Reading comprehension: Students search out specific types of quotes to illustrate metaphor, different styles of writing, humor, creativity, insight, etc.

Social studies: Ask for quotes to reflect particular points of views—for example, "Find one quote in the news that reflects optimism toward the world's future, and one that reflects pessimism." "Find three quotes each reflecting conservative viewpoints and liberal ones." Or leave the topic wide open.

Language arts, self-awareness, and creativity: Have students invent their own words of wisdom. Collect these into a class book. Or publish selected ones in the school newsletter. Or include them in letters to parents.

As an illustration of the versatility of quotations, we'll explore further the Winston Churchill quotation. From just this single quote you have a wide choice of related topics and activities:

> Vocabulary (optimist, pessimist)
> Leadership and empowerment: "To what extent is our attitude our own choice?"
> Journal writing: "Write about something you feel optimistic about."
> Role-play: Have students dramatize a specified situation from first an optimistic perspective, and then a pessimistic one.

■ METAPHOR AND ANALOGY

Metaphors stimulate our brains to make connections, engage our thinking, and expand our awareness. It is quite possible that metaphorical associations actually enhance brain functioning through increased numbers of nerve cell connections in the brain.

Metaphors have enormous power. Use them to increase students' comprehension of a new concept. You do this by (1) relating the new concept to a familiar one or (2) relating two familiar concepts, thus fostering a deeper perception of each.

Look at the ways in which the metaphor is accurate and the ways it is inaccurate. For example . . .

Science: Your brain is a computer. In what ways is this true? In what ways is this not true? Other science metaphors: A living cell is a country. The earth is a spaceship.

Literature: Find metaphors in literature. Have students create metaphors in their own writing.

Social problems: The metaphor creates distance, thus avoiding confrontation and defensive attitudes.

Creative Metaphors and Analogies

> "Which takes up more space, love or sound?"
> "Which is softer, a cloud or a whisper?"
> "Which is happier, a hug or a sunny day?"

Students in small groups can explore metaphorical comparisons such as those above. Groups then decide upon their answer and a reason why. There is obviously no single right answer. The sharing stimulates thinking, enhances whole brain associations of concepts and images, and can be immensely satisfying for certain styles of learners.

Self-awareness: Are you more like a sunrise or a sunset? An ocean, a pond, or a river? A salmon, a poodle, a butterfly, or some other animal? In what ways are you like . . . in what ways are you different? Which animal would you like to be? If you were a _____, how would you act, think, feel? If you could be any animal—or plant, insect, country, famous person—what would you be, and why?

You can follow up with sharing (as an icebreaker), discussion (lead-in to metaphors in poetry and literature), and writing (self-awareness focus).

Analogies for Thinking Skills

Example: "*Cake* is to *dessert* as *oak* is to *tree*."

There are many variations of analogies ranging from convergent to divergent, language to math to thinking skills. Using the simple format above, you can vary which of the four items is left blank. Or have students generate their own analogies to be shared with partners or the whole class. Use analogies to teach new material, as practice to help retention, or for thinking skills development.

Higher-level thinking: Encourage your students to go beyond the first right answer. Help them improve your analogy, and invent their own creative ones.

Visual/spatial skills: Analogies need not be verbal. Create and practice analogies with numbers, pictures, and objects.

Poetry: Use the analogies as a lead-in or raw material for writing poetry or paragraphs that expand upon the analogy.

Flash cards: The analogy with the answer is blank on one side, and the answer is on the other.

Cooperation, language arts, or humor: Develop a class analogies book.

▶ Creative Random Analogies

For highly creative and talented students, brainstormed words are randomly combined into incomplete analogies. Completion of the analogy almost always requires creative connections. The student explains the rationale for the chosen answer. (Here is an example of three words chosen randomly: "Paper is to air as tree is to _____." There is no specific correct answer; any answer with a reason is allowable. So, one possible answer to this one is "'Water,' because if I were an astronaut on another planet, I'd rather have air than paper, and I'd rather have water than a tree."

■ COLLABORATIVE WRITING

You can add a collaborative flair for variety and to build cooperative skills. Two examples are collaborative reports and class books.

Collaborative reports: Present a topic sentence stem to cooperative-learning groups. For example, "The main character is very realistic because . . ." Student A writes one sentence to complete the stem, students B and C add successive sentences that reinforce the topic sentence, and student D summarizes.

Class Books: For awareness and self-esteem, students collaboratively put together a book that includes their strengths, skills, and hobbies.

■ POETRY

Poetry stimulates visual imagery and feelings, whether through the writing of one's own poetry, or the reading and experiencing of another's. Poetry, of course, takes on many forms. The following are some creative and lesser-known variations to motivate your students.

Line-by-Line Poems

Provide a topic, sentence stem, or structure for each line. Here is a version of an autobiographical poem:

> First name: Justin
> Three adjectives to describe self: sociable, optimistic, athletic
> Brother or sister of: brother of John and Arthur,
> Lover of (three things): lover of basketball, lover of pizza, lover of traveling,
> Who needs, feels, gives, fears three things: who gives it all he's got, who feels too busy, who needs to win,
> Who would like: who would like peace for all
> Resident of: resident of Seattle, Washington
> Last name: Galen.

Yes, you can change it in so many ways. For example, design each line to review a historical character, fictional character, pet, favorite sport. Aha! Once kids get the idea after their first poem or two, why not work collaboratively with students to design the line-by-line structures.

Ice-breaking, rapport, self-awareness: Use at the beginning of the school year to learn about your students and for students to learn about each other. Publish one or more in the school newspaper.

Primary: Assign the poems as a homework assignment for a parent to do jointly with their child.

Language arts, creativity: Students create their own framework, and add additional verses.

Computer: Compose them on a computer using creative fonts.

Art, penmanship: Write them up with calligraphy pens.

Social studies, language arts, creativity: Create biographical poems for characters from novels or from history, or for current celebrities or political figures, or geographical places, or fictitious creatures of the imagination, or . . .

Collaborative Poems

Collaborative poetry is adapted from Kenneth Koch's wonderful book *Wishes, Lies and Dreams: Teaching Children to Write Poetry* (1999). Each individual writes only one line of the poem, and these separate lines are collected from the group and compiled into a single poem. A simple format is to begin with a sentence stem: "Spring is . . ." "Happiness is . . ." "I wish . . ." A similar variation requiring each student to contribute two lines begins "I used to . . ." and then continues "But now . . ." Collaborative poems are nonthreatening—any student can come up with one line!

Underachievers, at-risk learners, ESL, etc: One exciting benefit is that each student generally feels ownership and pride in the group's poem, even though he or she contributed only one line. Collaborative poems are quick to write, and they produce some interesting and entertaining results.

Lesson Closure: After you've taught a lesson on ecology, have your class write, "Ecology is . . ."

Motivate enjoyment of poetry: The ease and nonthreatening nature of this format can be used to entice learners to express themselves more willingly through poetry. Some of your students will quickly want to write not just one line but many.

Seed Poems

This novel technique produces some extraordinary poems in 15 minutes. Try it with your intermediate or middle school class, and, wow—you get some amazingly beautiful and creative results.

Here's the technique. You provide one word to the class (the "seed"), and each student must write a first line of a poem that includes that seed word anywhere in the line. After a couple of minutes, another seed word is given, and students then write a second line that contains this second word. Students do not know in advance what the next word will be, and they are to try and create a coherent flow among the separate lines they write. You can set the seed poem's length anywhere from four words and up. It's best to start with fewer lines so students can get used to the idea.

Here is an example of five seed words for a five-line poem: summer, music, tranquil, laughter, dessert.

Some of the poems will be outstanding; some will be nonsense. The joy of seed poems is that they enable students to quickly generate a creative poem in a matter of minutes. Students can fine-tune their poems afterwards if they like.

This spontaneous, creative burst of energy will produce a few poems that look like hours of work! Quite a number of students are thrilled that they had written the best poem of their lives in a mere 10 minutes. It has been for many students their favorite format for writing poetry.

■ JOURNAL-WRITING MENU

Create a diverse menu from which students may pick for their journaling. This menu can offer a variety of opportunities for *personal connection* to the student's interests, feelings, goals, and attitudes. For example:

> Personal discoveries, high points, low points, favorites (i.e., favorite ice cream flavor, favorite day of the year)
> "What is . . ." (i.e., what is love, what is a friend)
> "What if . . ." (i.e., what if everyone in the world were happy, what if there were no diseases, what if there were no night)
> "Imagine that you were . . ." (i.e., imagine you were a doctor, imagine you were president)
> "What age would you most like to be?" "What is it like being me? Write a poem titled 'Me'."

Be flexible so that students have opportunities to write and illustrate what they wish. A class journal can be assembled from data on each of the students; such data might include achievements, interests, summary of family, future goals, etc.

Freewrites

Students are given an exact amount of time, e.g., 3 minutes, to write quickly and spontaneously on a given topic.

Paired Sharing Journals

Students pair up to combine conversation with journal writing. You can either have them share first, followed by the journal writing, or write first, and then share what they wrote, either by reading their entry to their partner, letting their partner read it silently, or retelling what they wrote.

Chapter 8
An Appreciation for Quality

The following tools will help your students understand the nature of quality work, and want to produce that quality. See especially student self-assessment—this is rewarding for the children and can save you a great deal of time and effort.

■ RATE, EVALUATE, JUDGE (REJ)

Try to infuse your curriculum with many experiences so students can rate, evaluate, and judge various aspects of their learning. By doing so, you are (1) demonstrating acceptance, and therefore building students' self-concept; (2) fostering thinking skills; and (3) helping students become aware of, and accepting of, the various values among their peers.

William Glasser's concept of the quality school stresses how important it is for students to be aware of quality (Glasser, 1988). How can the concept of quality be learned if students do not have abundant opportunities to explore their opinions, to evaluate themselves, their learning, and their environment?

In its simplest form, this tool is nothing more than asking for your students' opinions. However, it is far more powerful for student thinking when children are also encouraged to have reasons for their ratings. In fact, to rate something according to criteria is a key attribute of critical thinking.

Applications for ratings are innumerable at any grade level and in any subject area. There are an endless variety of formats for REJs, such as the following:

Favorites: "Which type of pet would be your favorite? Why?" "Let's see which characters in the story are your favorites. And what makes that character interesting or special?"

Agree/disagree: "From the following list, put a 'yes' next to those with which you agree, and a 'no' next to those with you disagree."

Choice between two items: "Are people mostly generous or selfish?" "Would you describe school as interesting or boring?" "Are you more of a giver or a taker?"

Rank-order: "Rate the stories we read this week from '5' for your favorite, to '1' for your least favorite."

Multiple choice: "Which of the following movies would you most like to watch? ___ a horror movie; ___ a comedy; ___ a sci-fi adventure; ___ a romance."

Participation and ownership, learning and retention: Use this tool to facilitate student ownership of learning . . . reflection on values . . . dialogue among students . . . synthesis of content . . . and awareness of self and others. You can do these things with minimal additional planning. Students love to discuss their opinions, especially when there is more than one right answer. Use this tool repeatedly throughout the year with a wide range of lessons and projects.

Student initiative and empowerment: Have students make up their own lists for their peers to rate. The list might be of the various centers in a kindergarten classroom or a list of sports or music.

Lesson starters, practice: Ratings work well as lead-ins to a unit or lesson focusing on either content or process skills, as icebreakers to warm up a group and build rapport, and for practice. "Here are three different story problems. Rate them from easiest to hardest, and tell why?"

Closure: "Now that we have finished our entire science unit, let's pick out our favorite and least favorite activities, and talk about which ones we learned the most, or the least."

Self-awareness (intermediate grades and above): First, brainstorm with students the traits and attitudes that enable a person to succeed in life. Second, students can rate the list in the following two ways:

- Order the list according to which items are most important (at the top) to least important (at the bottom).
- Place an "S" next to items that are strengths and an "I" next to items that need more improvement.

Social studies and science: The format for ratings can be a simple list, or it can take the form of more elaborate grids, tables, or graphs. These latter formats lend themselves marvelously to grouping the data for easy interpretation for the entire class.

Geography: After your class has brainstormed and researched a list of thirty countries in the world, ask them to rate each from favorite to least favorite according to where they would want to live. Students must justify their ratings in terms of criteria—climate, politics, economy, language, culture, and other differences.

Values Tasks

Here are more examples that encourage students to explore their values—to rate, evaluate, and judge.

Language arts: "Write about someone important to you." "List the characters in the novel from your favorite to least favorite, and explain why you rated them that way."

Tests: Include questions on your exams such as "Which parts of the chapter did you like more/less? Explain why." "What part(s) of this unit do you think you will use in your life?" (Answers to each of the questions would count as part of the total grade. Accept any legitimate answer.)

Critical thinking skills: Have students articulate the reasoning behind their opinions. For example, ask your class which sports or hobbies are their favorites, then proceed to discussion: "Why is that your favorite?"

Self-awareness: "Which of the following is most important? (1) To be happy (2) To have money (3) To have friends (4) To have confidence"

Voting

By calling it voting, you add a real-world relevance to it. In its simplest form, have students raise their hands to vote. Or it can be in the form of a written questionnaire, with several or more items.

Social studies: "At what age do you believe people should be allowed to vote in this country? Why?" Discussion can lead in to our political system, how a democracy works, or how opinion polls are designed.

Thinking skills, graphing, and data analysis: Vote on the best soft drink. Tabulate the returns so they can be presented in table or graph form. But don't stop here—have students interpret the data in the same way that students are asked to interpret data from a science experiment. What conclusions can be drawn? Could the questionnaire be improved to yield more clear-cut results? Would it be interesting to sample a different population (i.e., another classroom or grade level)? What are our predicted outcomes if we did this?

Younger children for self-awareness, team-building, leadership: "Which of the following lunch items is your favorite?" "Is it better to have a big dog, small dog, or no dog?" Have students be in charge of a "vote of the week," in which one team of students surveys their peers each week.

■ Criteria Setting

Teach children how to identify the criteria that underlie quality. One cannot rationally rate or evaluate anything without first having established criteria.

Introduce the skill of criteria setting with a playful, student-centered item to evaluate. Ask students "What makes a good bicycle?" Or "What makes a great pet?" You can make it even more fun and hands-on by bringing in three or four brands of chocolate-chip cookies. Develop criteria for rating the cookies (e.g., taste, texture, chips), then have students sample half a cookie of each brand, and record a rating (from one to three). When several items are being rated according to several criteria, it lends itself nicely to also introducing students to an organized decision-making matrix or data table. Ask students how to judge friendship, success, happiness, justice.

Motivation, ownership, learning: When students are involved in establishing relevant criteria, their learning and retention are enhanced enormously. By all means, involve students in a discussion of the criteria by which their assignments and their grade are assessed.

Homework assignments, projects: With any assignment, if students understand the criteria, they can work to meet those criteria.

Language arts: Brainstorm with students the criteria that make a good story, or a good essay, or good penmanship, or a good oral presentation. Or "What makes a great day?" Take the brainstormed criteria, and have students write a paragraph or story titled "The Best Day."

Social studies: Brainstorm criteria that make a good leader, or an effective government. Then use those criteria to evaluate leaders and governments you are studying.

Design criteria for quality, and assess with those criteria. Help kids develop detailed mental pictures of what they are striving to learn or produce. Let students take part in creating the assessment criteria so they have comprehension and ownership of those criteria. Children are capable of creating criteria with you. They'll do higher-quality work with more intrinsic motivation, and be competent at self-assessment.

■ STUDENT SELF-ASSESSMENTS

Student self-assessments are an essential cluster of tools—ones that should be an active part of every teacher's repertoire. In fact, they are so effective and versatile that they tend to become quite habit-forming. They just could be one of the best investments you can make in your teaching repertoire.

Once these tools become a more automatic part of your teaching, you will be amazed that you once lived without them! However, it does generally take some trial and error to fine-tune for your teaching style and your students, so start small.

Steps for Self-assessment

Do your students know how their efforts and products are being scored or graded? Do they know, for example, whether spelling counts, or creativity, or neatness? Do *you* know exactly what you are looking for?

Here are the steps for using student self-assessments for a wide range of assignments and projects.

Step 1: Think about exactly what criteria are most essential to this task. The criteria should be as authentic as possible. In other words, these should be the facets of the task that are most valued by real people in the real world.

Step 2: Tell your students! It is crucial that students know what you are looking for. Get rid of the surprises—if spelling doesn't count, tell them. Better yet, discuss the possible criteria with the students. Build a collaborative trusting, relationship in which you and the students together arrive at meaningful criteria.

Make it concrete: Find or create actual examples to assess with your students—perhaps you have student work from a prior year; just white out the name.

Step 3: Students self-assess according to the criteria you (and they) have agreed upon. You may want to have students include reasons explaining each score they arrived at for each criterion. Additionally, you will find it quite fruitful to have students describe parts that could be improved.

Step 4: You assess students' work. Where you go from here depends on you. You need to decide what to do with the students' self-assessments.

What Next . . .

You'll get three possible results:

> **1.** The student may have assessed the work lower than you did.
> **2.** The student thinks he or she did better than you think.
> **3.** The student and you agree on the same assessed score.

If student self-assessed lower than you did: This frequently happens, especially with your more dedicated learners. This is valuable information for you. It means perhaps that the student has very high expectations, or perhaps that he or she does not understand the criteria or the levels of quality associated with those criteria. It may be that the student knows he or she is capable of even better. It frequently means that the student seeks to be honest with him or herself. Or it may indicate the student is too hard on himself or herself.

According to the particular reason for the discrepancy between your scores and the students, you have valuable information and an opportunity to further dialogue with the student to build greater trust or improve learning.

If student self-assessed higher than you did: This is a common occurrence. This is a predictable result when the student is either ignorant of the levels of quality expected, or hopes to deceive you into giving a higher grade. With further experience, students' self-assessments match your own with increasing frequency. What a wonderful outcome—for students to learn to recognize the quality of what they are doing, and to understand what they can do better.

Student's self-assessment is same as yours: Yes! Yes! Now, you've arrived. And perhaps surprisingly, this result is very achievable. When the criteria are clear, when the trust and accountability are present, kids are remarkably accurate at judging quality.

A Summary of the Benefits

There are splendid reasons why you want to use student self-assessments:

Improved student success: Students become more attuned to the quality of their work, and the specific criteria that make for quality.

Improved student attitude: Students and teacher can readily see and communicate which aspects of a particular work are in need of improvement, and students are more likely to then make those improvements. Students feel ownership of their work and feel empowered to take control of their grades. They know where their grades come from, and what they can do to improve them.

Your stress is less: Students see you as an ally, not an adversary. You become partners in the quest for quality. You are no longer the unjust person who "gave" the student the low grade.

Your workload is less: The more that you use this tool, the fewer comments you need to write on students' work. This is because the student has already written the very same comment! I find it quite a time-saver to merely circle the student's self-assessed scores when those scores match what I would have given for each criterion.

Self-assessments of Feelings and Attitudes

Students can self-assess how they feel about an activity, about a school day, about themselves. They can rate their attitudes, their effort, and their experiences.

The assessment can be numerical ratings (e.g., 1–5), or for primary students, try happy and sad faces. You can create a questionnaire or inventory form, or you can have your students share orally.

Chapter 9
Collaboration and Celebration

Entire books exist on cooperative learning and the instructional tools to facilitate it. Rather than explore cooperative learning strategies in depth, we will sample just a few readily implemented tools. Likewise, from cooperation emerges a joyful community that deserves celebration. These celebrations need not be complicated or time-consuming.

■ FOSTERING COLLABORATION

A cooperative classroom is made up of cooperative individuals who enjoy school enough to want to behave responsibly toward other human beings. Explicit use of cooperative learning does not make a cooperative classroom. It is the atmosphere of the class more than the instructional strategy that nurtures cooperation.

A positive, caring, relevant learning environment is the starting point. You won't accomplish much cooperative learning in a classroom devoid of rapport among students and teacher. And try not to use cooperative learning for tasks that are best accomplished individually.

Peer-to-Peer Support

A number of years ago, I had a 7th grade student who was insecure, withdrawn, and new to public education. She had been home-schooled and had been diagnosed with mild learning problems. During the first week of school, I asked her if there was any other student in the class who she felt comfortable talking to if she had questions. She volunteered a couple of names, and I checked with one of those students, who was very happy to help. (Human beings love to be helpers, except where unhealthy social environments have obliterated this natural tendency.)

The outcome was this: (1) I cut my workload, because this student was now less dependent upon me; (2) the child had a peer as a friend and support person, which builds self-esteem and enjoyment of learning; and (3) this girl was now academically more successful, thus nurturing her continuing and accelerating efforts and successes. Interestingly, by the end of the year, this girl had made such enormous progress in learning, in attitude, and in confidence, that I became forever convinced that the "power of relationship" is a crucial foundation for any classroom. This *must* be one of your highest priorities for the first month of school, and for each month following.

Cross-Age Collaboration

Explore opportunities for cooperation or tutoring across grade levels.

Tutoring: Older students can tutor younger ones. What about at-risk high school students helping younger children at the elementary school? The sources of tutors include retired persons, community members, and university students.

Empowering at-risk learners: What about having your struggling, or low self-esteem, 4th graders reading to first graders?

Class presentations: Students from one class can visit another to present a motivating lesson. How about having 1st graders visit a 5th grade classroom to dazzle with simple magic tricks?

Cooperative Role Definition

When students work in small groups for tasks or projects, define the roles for each group member. For example, person A rephrases directions, B is recorder/note-taker, C is facilitator/praiser to keep things moving smoothly, D is timekeeper.

The more complex the group task, the more authentic is the cooperative role definition. In the real world, workers have specific roles designed to ensure more effective completion of each task. Each person specializes on a part of the whole while communication and leadership skills glue the parts together.

Turn to a Neighbor

Periodically, have your students each turn to a partner to respond to a question or topic. It's quick, and it fosters alertness.

Playful, positive classroom climate: "Turn to a neighbor, smile, and wish them good luck." "Turn to your neighbor, and ask them what they are having for lunch."

Learning, retention: This provides an opportunity for each student to actively participate, even though it only takes 10–30 seconds. "Turn to a neighbor, and point in your notes [or the paragraph in the textbook, etc.] to the main idea we've been discussing." "Turn to your partner and summarize the procedure for our science experiment today."

Formative assessment: "Turn to a neighbor and tell them the three main characters in this novel." In this example, as you listen in on the sharing you can quickly assess the students' comprehension.

Paired Sharing

Students in pairs are given a particular topic to discuss. One partner shares while the other listens, and then they switch. While A is speaking, B shall maintain eye contact, and listen without speaking.

Pairs of Pairs

This is a simple two-step process. Students first work in pairs, and then two pairs group together (forming groups of four) to share and compare their work, or to proceed with the next step in the task. For example, pairs could brainstorm questions related to a particular topic, while the pairs of pairs could follow-up with organizing the questions or conducting research to find the answers.

Round Robin

Students are in groups of four or five. Starting with one student, each group member in turn responds to a question or topic, with the responses proceeding around the circle until each member has contributed.

Collaborative Displays: Wall Hangings, Murals, Collages, Quilts

Each student is allocated one square section of the whole classroom to design. This can be a one-time activity, or you can arrange for students to add to and modify their square throughout the school year. Their design might include artwork, photos, or examples of their work.

This is an open-ended project to facilitate students' awareness and acceptance of each other's uniqueness, to build team spirit, and to encourage students' ownership of their classroom.

Social studies/science: The focus of the display can be a particular content area. For example, for a life science unit, each student can choose one animal and design the square to communicate that animal's uniqueness, beauty, or ecological relationships. Or each square might depict one of our fifty states.

■ Sharing Circles

Students form a circle, either one large one, or several smaller ones. Each student in turn shares a thought with the group. Some categories for sharing include favorite moment of the month, one word to describe the day, what I like about myself, or most meaningful or enjoyable experience of the year.

Try the topic "What I Learned Today." Then when students return home and a parent asks, "What did you learn today?"—the student will know!

Sharing circles are excellent for closure at the end of the day or unit. When students connect their content knowledge with their values and feelings, retention is far greater. Give your students a chance to become more aware of each other—to see their individual uniqueness as well as their shared experiences.

You may also like to try the following variations of the sharing circle.

Sharing Pairs

Students are in pairs, with partners sharing positive thoughts, experiences, memories, etc. The teacher may direct the students' sharing by specifying a theme, such as a trip, a close friend, a humorous incident, a favorite time spent with an animal, or a most enjoyable moment in school.

Images Circle

Several or more students sit in a circle. One object is placed in the hands of a student; that child must share thoughts or feelings (i.e., images) related to the object until the teacher says "Pass," at which time the object goes to the right, the next student talks about the object until "pass," and so on. The one constraint—which makes it interesting—is that no student may repeat what any other person in the circle has said already.

Review, reinforcement of learning: Use image circles to review content in a playful, open-ended way—at the end of a unit on rocks, for example, much of their learning will be shared as a rock continues around the circle. Or after reading a story, pass the book around the circle to hear student reactions.

Social skills: Foster listening and observation skills, patience and perseverance; provide a discussion format where each person can be heard.

Thinking skills: Motivate imagination, metaphors, and analogies.

Language skills: Expand students' vocabulary of adjectives and generate ideas for writing assignments.

Variations: Talk to the object, not about it. Talk about a word or an experience, or a photograph/drawing.

Frequently, as the object (or word) progresses around the circle, the shared thoughts grow in creativity, and begin to incorporate more senses, more abstract and personal reactions, etc. Thus, the full range of responses enhances our awareness of ourselves as "whole" beings (both right-brained and left, sensory and thinking, serious and humorous). Image circles are well suited as a lesson starter, as an informal pre-test, as a self-awareness/sharing session, or as review and closure (adapted from Van Matre, 1972).

Question Circle

This activity is similar to the images circle, but is more teacher-mediated. Students are in a circle, one student having a symbolic card or object that gives only the person holding it the right to speak. Begin by asking an open-ended question, such as "What is a friend?" or "What do we mean when we say we should be good?" The student with the card speaks until he or she chooses to pass the card to the next person. That person may speak or say "Pass." The teacher may change or clarify the question at any point in the circle, to facilitate productive sharing.

This is a useful way to encourage students to listen to each other, to express thoughts and feelings without being judged by the teacher, to be aware of choices, and to enable quieter students to have an opportunity to speak. This activity is a productive one for class meetings. Consider splitting the class into two or more smaller circles to facilitate more student participation.

Sharing Circle with Movement

This is an active, out-of-seat version of a sharing circle. It is an excellent sharing activity for younger children because the movement keeps them involved and attentive.

Everyone forms a circle by holding hands, and rotates slowly to the left. Any child may call "Stop" to freeze the group. Then that child shares a special feeling or appreciation, followed by calling "Go." Upon hearing "Go," the group switches direction, circling to the right, till the next person calls "Stop." This continues until all who want to share have done so. If 10 seconds or so go by with nobody sharing, then everyone rushes to the center of the circle to give himself or herself a giant standing ovation (adapted from Weinstein and Goodman, 1980).

■ GROUPING AND LINING-UP TOOLS

If you ever have students work in groups, or line up, you'll enjoy some of the creative alternatives discussed in the following paragraphs. You might create new groups prior to an academic task, or simply to foster a positive classroom atmosphere.

Line-Up Games

Add some playful variety to the task of lining up. If you are a bit creative, you will see how the following activities can be used for teaching cooperative behavior, reviewing of months, fostering self-awareness, encouraging kids to interact with a wider range of peers.

Birthday line-ups: The children must line up in birthday order without speaking. They signal their birthday by holding up fingers—one for January, nine for September, and so forth. Once they find their place in line according to month order, they work on the day in the same fashion.

Height line-ups: With eyes closed, the children try to get into height order. This is done by gently patting their neighbors' heads to find their proper place in line.

Preference line-ups: "Rate how much you like chocolate from *one* (strong dislike) to *ten* (your favorite food). Now get in order, with tens over here and ones at this end."

Signal Groupings

There are a variety of playful ways to break students up into different groupings, either as a community-building activity, or for an academic task that will follow.

Random handshake groups: "Pick a number, either 1, 2, or 3. Don't tell anyone your number. Now get out of your seats, and without talking, shake other people's hands. If you're a one, shake once. If a two, shake twice, and so on. You'll be able to feel when your number matches the other person's. Stay together with anyone having the same number. Remember, no talking. You have 60 seconds for ones to be with ones, twos with twos, and threes with threes."

Nose-taps and vowels: You can use other signals besides handshaking. You can try nose taps or ear tugs, for example. "Count how many vowels are in your last name. Now, without talking, find others in the class with the same number of vowels by tapping on your nose that same number. You have 60 seconds to form your groups."

Content connections: You can use any number of criteria to review academic concepts:

> "Shake the number of syllables in the name of your favorite animal." (syllables review).
> "Ear-tug your favorite month." (1 = January, 2 = February, etc.)

As follow-up, have the groups share with each other what they like about that month. Then have students write a composition related to something about their favorite month.

■ Awards, Mottoes, Contests, and Celebrations

Here's a diverse collection. If you can't find something you like here, then (1) invent your own, or (2) have students invent a new version.

Creative Awards

Awards are used throughout the business world to support and motivate employees. In education, we have the standard awards for high grades and good attendance. Why not get a little creative and invent some new awards? Of course, there is no reason at all why children cannot be involved in this process of invention.

If your budget is limited, you'll appreciate "invisible prizes." These are quite inexpensive, easy to store, and can be fabricated instantaneously. I had 6th graders actually thinking up the idea of paying me invisible money for their invisible prize. You'll just have to put on a good act as you haul this invisible 6-foot-tall gold trophy through the doorway. Perhaps your class can design a wide selection of other imaginary prizes.

"Fastest Grower Award": Award this to the child who gains the most height between September and June.

Smile awards: Establish categories and criteria, such as "most continual smile," "most teeth missing smile," "most twinkle-in-the-eye smile," "friendliest smile."

"Micro Print Award": Give this to the student who can write the smallest legibly.

"Master of Doodling Degree, MD": This is for students who show enormous potential in this vital area.

"Golden Broom Award": Award this to students or teams who demonstrate the greatest proficiency for keeping the room clean.

Secret Pals (Dedications Ceremonies)

Each student dedicates a "present" to another individual whose name was picked out of a hat. The present can be a poem, story, or inexpensive object. All names are kept secret till the dedications ceremony.

"Secret Pals" is a joyful celebration of positive group feelings in any class that already has a positive team climate. However, it can backfire if you've got a divisive or apathetic group. As with all else, use your judgment.

Lottery Tickets

There is serious and valid debate about the merits of giving out stickers, stars, and other extrinsic rewards. If you are going to do it, lottery tickets are one fruitful possibility. Give students tickets for a specified positive deed—grades or positive behavior, for example. Tickets are collected, and one or more are drawn as winners. The reward for winning can be whatever you have decided.

Hot tip: Lottery tickets enable you to get by with fewer rewards, because out of every twenty or fifty tickets given to students, there are only one or two winners. You decide the ratio. The random aspect of the drawing is motivating in itself.

Class Names

Agree on a class name—Porpoises, or Explorers, or Rutabagas. Your class might be the only Rutabaga team in the country! Create a logo.

Mottoes and Mini-rituals

By all means, you and your students should generate a class motto. Kids really enjoy this. Here's one shared by self-esteem expert Michele Borba: "Of all the people in the world, I'm special, I'm a thumb body." (Students recite this while holding their fist out, thumb up.)

Standing Ovation

Any person may ask for a standing ovation. The group then gives that person stupendous cheers and applause, and the person demonstrates proud acceptance of the acknowledgment. You may even encourage more than one person (or even much of the group) to simultaneously get a standing ovation. This is a wonderful self-esteem builder, likely to be remembered for some time!

You can manage the standing ovations in this way: each student may request a card, entitling them to a standing ovation that week. When a student wants the ovation, he or she hands the card to the teacher, who then gives the OK at the next appropriate moment during class. In this way, you can schedule them at the end of the period or day, and avoid any disruptions.

Celebrations

You can celebrate anything. Kids are always in the mood for a party!
Curriculum: Design a celebration for authors, characters in books, or events.
Creativity: Plan to celebrate . . . the discovery of onions, the invention of pencil erasers. Students can create skits, songs, artwork, or poems—anything at all that is in the spirit of the celebration.

Chapter 10
Your Playful Repertoire

■ SELF-SORTING

Call out criteria by which students move to specified places in the room. For example, "If you like chocolate ice cream, stand over here. If you prefer vanilla ice cream, stand over there. If you don't like either, stand by the window." You might want to sort by birthdays, number of siblings, color of clothing items, interests, opinions, or life experiences.

This visual/spatial/kinesthetic activity enables students to see patterns far more readily than if individuals merely raise their hands to indicate their attributes. Furthermore, students themselves can call out the criterion for grouping, thereby learning about many aspects of their peers of interest to them, as well as developing leadership skills.

Community building: Because the children are grouped with others that share something in common, you have spent a few minutes helping build a greater sense of community.

Motivation, transition times: Students are out of their seats and moving—the physical movement alone may help stimulate motivation and learning, and to refocus them to begin the next task.

Math: You can tally the numbers in each sorting and create bar graphs. Convert them into fractions or percentages. Unlike math problems in the book, these will be real for the kids—and therefore, both more interesting and more concrete.

Icebreaker or needs assessment: Use it as an icebreaker for district-wide inservices, or for parents at open house. Use criteria that will provide useful information—e.g., by interest or concern or goals.

■ OBSERVATION GAMES

Children love to observe—sure beats writing for many of them! Therefore, let a variety of observation activities and games be an avenue to engage kids at the start of a lesson or unit. Let the observations lead to the concepts and skills. Alternatively, observation tasks are superb as review or closure to any unit. The skills and concepts you taught will enable your students to demonstrate (and celebrate) their learning via their more detailed and astute observations. Thus, you have another assessment tool in your repertoire that is performance-based in a modality other than writing.

Find Your Own

Distribute one apple—or rock, or popcorn kernel—to each student. Children must now observe their items as closely as possible. After a few minutes, clusters of students place their items together on a desk, and each student must now find his or her original item. Start with easier items the first round, so success is assured.

Art or language: Instead of just observing their items, students draw and/or describe them in writing. The drawings or descriptions are randomly distributed among the students, who must find the item that matches the drawing they received.

Math: Similar to above, only students' descriptions must be accurate measurements of their object's dimensions. Use objects such as pencils and pens of various dimensions; a variety of nails, screws, etc, from your garage; leaves from your yard; small rocks.

Sensory Box

This is the well-known activity whereby an unknown object is placed in a box or bag, accessible to the students' touch—you can add smell or taste—but not sight. You have a fun change of pace for your more tactile learners.

Communication skills: The student feeling the object describes that object's attributes to a partner, who must either identify the object by name, or draw it. Or you might place in the box a number of similar objects, such as nuts and bolts. The pair of students must communicate well enough that one partner can retrieve the correct object based upon his her partner's descriptions.

Primary level, the senses, vocabulary words: Use objects with various shapes, textures, smells, sounds. This "discovery box" can be a regular feature of a science center. Change the objects frequently. Put kids in charge of this project. Each child can have his or her own discovery box—who can come up with the most surprising mystery object?

Changes Game

Students pair up. One partner turns her back, while the other secretly changes five aspects of his appearance (e.g., untying shoe, brushing hair differently, changing body posture). The partner then attempts to observe what changes were made.

Skills and attributes of this game include observation and team-building enjoyment.

Observation Memory Game

In a covered box is a collection of miscellaneous items (e.g., plastic spoon, light bulb, rock, cereal box). The items are placed in plain view on a desktop for 5 minutes, during which time students are to observe all items carefully. Items are then taken out of view, and returned to the box. Questions are asked: "List each of the items." "What kind of cereal was it?"

Reinforce previously learned concepts: The observation memory game is practice/reinforcement for items or words studied; just place in the box pictures or word cards of the content you want the students to practice for improved retention.

Lesson starter for introducing brain-based learning concepts: You might also relate this activity to such process skills as observing, long- and short-term memory, and mnemonics.

Patterns/math: Place a simple pattern of objects on a table (e.g., three each of different shape—square, circular, triangular, etc.). Let students observe closely to look for patterns. Then cover up the objects, and remove one. The purpose of the game is for the students to guess the object that was removed.

People observation game: Ask the class to observe one student for a minute or two. That individual then leaves the room. The remaining students then write down observations they recall about the individual, such as color, pattern, and style of clothes, shoes, and hair.

■ "What's My Rule" Games

In these games, the group tries to guess a rule known only to the leaders. Most obviously, they are wonderful motivators when you have a few spare moments. There are solidly academic and standards-driven uses for these as well.

Secret Sorting

The leader has in mind a secret criterion for sorting all of the students into two or more groups. The leader starts the game by pointing to any student and directing that individual to an area of the room. One student after another is directed to their appropriate place—generally two or three different groups being formed—though only the "sorter" knows what criterion is being used to sort the group. As the as-yet ungrouped students observe the growing groups, these students can guess to which group they think they belong.

"Secret sorting" provides a playful experience with concepts such as grouping, critical attributes, and observation skills. Students are not to share out loud what the sorting criteria might be.

Some possible criteria include eye color, clothing patterns, type of shoes, laced vs. unlaced shoes, straight vs. wavy/curly hair.

Team building: New interactions among students are enhanced, as the children find themselves in novel groupings, rather than with their usual friends.

Activity reward, self-esteem: For younger kids, mystery sorting is a nice out-of-seat break, and it's a marvelous esteem-builder for the child who gets to be the sorter.

Primary level math: A pleasant lesson to reinforce classification, patterns, and thinking skills. You can graph the results.

Awareness, observation, thinking skills: Young children become more aware of how they are similar to and different from others. It also motivates their perseverance with problem-solving.

Tillie Williams

Tell your students that Tillie Williams is a very interesting person who has particular likes and dislikes. The students are to figure out what she might like and dislike from the examples you give. "She likes carrots, but not peas," "She likes floors, but not tables," etc. The rule in this case is that she likes all words with double letters.

Vary Tillie's criteria to teach/reinforce a wide variety of concepts.

Note-taking, data collection and analysis: Require that students record the data in two columns, and search for the critical attribute that distinguishes the two sets.

Geography: "Tillie likes Paris, but not Boston." (foreign vs. U.S. cities)
Nutrition: "Tillie likes peas, but not apples." (vegetables vs. fruits)
Math: "Tillie likes 3 but not 8." (odd vs. even numbers)
Spelling, grammar, history, characters in stories, EVERYTHING: If you can split something into two lists—examples and non-examples—you can use Tillie Williams to reinforce attributes of a concept!

Safari or Picnic

The leader has an unstated rule as to what can be brought on the safari (or picnic). Everyone tries to figure out the rule by testing a variety of examples, to which the leader responds with "yes" or "no." For example:

"We're going on a safari, and I'm going to bring an apple. Does anyone else want to come?"

"Yes, I do. Can I bring a snowball?"

"No."

"Can I bring a peach?"

"Yes." (In this case, the rule is that any fruit can be brought.)

Use "Safari" to reinforce attributes and grouping, and as a playful review of many concepts.

Self-esteem and empowerment: Let students lead their peers through their own versions of this and other games. Students thus empowered will learn to take greater ownership of their learning, will exhibit increased initiative, and develop their self-esteem.

Primary grades: Take first an apple, then a ball, proceeding alphabetically. Or each day, children can bring any and all words beginning with that day's letter—see which letter-days make the biggest picnic!

Note-taking, thinking skills, hypothesizing: Pick a more difficult rule, and encourage students to record two columns of notes on what can and cannot be brought on the safari. Their thinking challenge is to test their hypotheses as they study their data.

A Note on Choosing Student Volunteers

There are a variety of games in which the teacher chooses a student partner—an accomplice—to perform a simple magic trick for the class. For example, see the "secret code games" that follow. Choose a student who needs attention, would excel at the game, might get a boost to self-image, is often unsuccessful in class, or is going through a difficult time in life. Or, share a game with one or two students who are leaders, and they will share it with friends (hence, kids teaching kids).

Secret Code Games

In these games, two partners have devised some secret way of communicating information. The audience is to guess how they do it.

▸ Secret Code Version #1

This trick requires two accomplices who have secretly agreed beforehand on a simple way for one partner (person A) to cue the answer to the other (person B). Person B leaves the room while the class picks an object in the room. When B returns, person A will use their secret cue (unknown to their peers) to communicate the correct object.

For example, the cue could be when person A uses the word "this" when speaking to person B. Thus, A asks, "Is it the wall?" Partner B answers, "No." "Is it the chalkboard? "No." "Is it *this* pencil?" And partner B instantly knows to answer "Yes." The partners can agree beforehand on any one of a thousand cues. The cue can be visual (person A puts left hand in pocket); or auditory (person A uses the word "this" when pointing to the correct object). The cue can also be an attribute of the objects being pointed to; for example, the correct object will be the one immediately following any object pointed to that is blue. And finally—my favorite—it can be an arithmetic sequence. The first time you do it, it will be the second object, then the fourth, then the sixth, and so on.

▸ Secret Code Version #2

Person A leaves the classroom while the class chooses a word from a particular category (e.g., fruits, animals, etc). Person A returns, and person B, using a yardstick or pointer, draws mysterious—and meaningless—patterns on the floor, as person A silently watches. Person A within a minute or two readily guesses the correct word. The secret is that person B has communicated the word, letter by letter, to person A. The first letter of each verbalization by person A indicates in sequence each letter of the secret word. Thus, if the animal to be guessed is "rabbit," person B will first say something like "Ready?" indicating "R." Then, person B draws some meaningless patterns, says "Second clue," and then "Are you ready"—the "A" from "Are you ready" indicating the second letter of "rabbit." Continue till person A guesses the animal.

Self-esteem, rapport: This is a motivating "filler" and more. Choose as your co-conspirator a student deserving of a reward or positive attention or improved self-esteem—this will make the student's day!

Science, observation skills: I've used this activity many times to get middle school kids to hypothesize, collect data, and test hypotheses through more observations. They love the playful nature of the game, and they learn how to hypothesize. Plus, I have nothing to photocopy and nothing to collect and grade!

Do-as-I-Do Games

One example, Johnny Oops, should readily illustrate this observation game. Johnny Oops is an entertaining game for any age. Though simple and quite silly, it does involve observation skills and creative problem-solving.

To play Johnny Oops, hold your right hand up, fingers spread. With your left index finger lightly tap each finger of right hand in turn, beginning with the pinkie, saying "Johnny" with each tap, and then "Oops" as you slide your left index finger down and back up to the next finger. Continue this to the right thumb, and then back to the pinkie, alternately saying "Oops" and "Johnny" at the appropriate times. As soon as you are done, immediately cross your arms. Ask students, "Do what I did." The key is for the students to cross their arms when they finish. Most kids will not catch on to this, because they focus so exclusively only on the finger movements.

Johnny Oops is fun to do as an activity reward or filler, and is a pleasant, fairly structured opportunity to play and laugh.

Thinking skills, social studies, science: Johnny Oops does illustrate how easy it is to see only what we want to see, and is a simulation of so many occasions in human history whereby the truth is in plain view, yet invisible. Thus, it took scientists years to discover that radioactive radon gas was perhaps the second leading cause of lung cancer—nobody had thought to look at the air we breathe. Likewise, it took years for geologists to accept the theory of plate tectonics (i.e., continental drift) because it was just too difficult to accept that continents might move—even though the evidence was right there for all geologists to see.

Preconceived ideas prevent each of us from seeing reality as it is. Centuries ago many European explorers actually thought that the blacks in Africa did not have language! We see only what we choose to see, or what we are conditioned to look for.

■ Magic and Fantasy

We all need a bit of fantasy and imagination. Perhaps this is one reason for the popularity of fairy tales, animated cartoons, and science fiction movies.

Fantasy Guests

If you have a bit of theatrics within you, you can quickly incorporate some fantasy merely by adding a bit of costume and changing your voice—be an explorer, a frog, a storybook character. Let this fantasy add an aliveness and novelty to the routines of teaching on-going content and skills . . . sight words, grammar rules, math facts. Interestingly, you can predictably immerse students within the same fantasy whenever you teach that particular content. In effect, you are enabling the kids to have the variety of a second "teacher."

Here are a couple of examples to illustrate the diverse applications of magic and fantasy. These do far more than just entertain, as you'll see.

Mysterious Footprints

Footprints are one primary-level example. Make mysterious footprints lead out a window, or into a closet. Lead a visualization in conjunction with the footprints to stimulate students' vivid imagery. Primary children can discuss what type of animal made the footprints, how it can be caught, and what it might eat. Use the footprints to teach attributes, symmetry, spatial relationships, and problem-solving.

Math: Students can measure the length of the mystery footprints and their stride, compare them to their own, and hypothesize the size of the animal based upon the concept of proportions.

Whole language: For art and creative writing, students can create a story, with a picture of the animal, and write a description of how to design or build a trap for the animal. Follow-up with students by reading stories with imaginary creatures. A creative teacher has many opportunities here to motivate children.

Invisible Glue (Magic Bottle with String)

A piece of rope amazingly appears to get instantly glued inside a bottle by "invisible glue." To perform the magic, secretly place a small, tightly crumpled paper ball inside any bottle having a tapered neck (e.g., a wine bottle). Cover the bottle with spray paint, tape, or aluminum foil so that one cannot see inside. You will also need a 12-inch piece of thick, stiff rope.

To do the magic act, take out your imaginary jar of "invisible glue," dip the rope into the glue, and then place the end of the rope into the bottle. When you tip the bottle upside down, the ball rolls down to lodge against the rope in the constriction of the bottle's neck. Thus, you can let go of the rope, and it hangs from the bottle as if glued in place. You can even flip it back up, enabling the bottle to hang from the string. As with any good magic, there are many classroom applications for this simple trick.

Thinking skills/problem-solving: Students guess/predict/create the mechanism that holds the string.

Art: Students creatively draw what is inside the bottle.

Creative writing: Students describe the glue's discovery, and how it will change the world; a story about invisible glue.

Science: This is a good lead-in motivator (anticipatory set) for a lesson on technological change and inventions. Of course, invisible glue does not really exist, but then, 200 years ago, neither did light bulbs, or planes, computers, or trips to the moon.

The Elmer variation: Often, I let the students know that it isn't glue at all; it's my little friend, Elmer, who lives inside the bottle. Elmer's job is to hold onto the rope when I tell him to.

Language arts with Elmer: We create imaginary interviews with Elmer and write about Elmer's life, how he ended up with this job, what he does for hobbies.

■ HUMOR

A good dose of humor reduces stress, heightens alertness and creativity, and boosts self-esteem. And obviously, it makes us happier.

Teach Positive vs. Negative Humor

The two types of humor: Teach kids the differences between the two types of humor. With positive humor, we are all laughing "with." Negative humor is a laughing "at." Positive humor feels good for everyone, builds team spirit, and breaks down barriers between people. Negative humor—which includes sarcasm, insults, and ridicule—is at someone's expense, hurts self-esteem, and breaks teams apart.

Notice the humor in your classroom: What humor is present? Is there positive humor each and every day? If necessary, plan ways to incorporate humor more regularly. Post on your wall some clever sayings or funny comics. Introduce a lesson with a humorous anecdote. Smile. Laugh at yourself.

Class humor book: Keep a class book of favorite jokes, puns, and riddles. Publish this at the end of the year. Ask your students to share funny things that happened to them.

Reading, speaking: Provide one or more books of jokes for students to skim during their free time. Students volunteer to share one of their favorite jokes at the end of the day.

Rapport, speaking skills, self-esteem: Have students share puns and riddles; encourage them to practice their joke-telling abilities in front of their peers.

Creativity, self-awareness, language arts: Pose questions such as "Do animals have a sense of humor?" "Is a sense of humor important? In what ways?" "What would an orange find humorous? What does your dog find humorous?" Follow up these questions with discussion or writing assignments.

■ TASK ROTATIONS

This is a playful and motivating way to complete a task, such as worksheets, textbook questions, or creative writing. Students rotate one desk—or learning station—at a time around the room, working on the assignment or worksheet at the desk in front of them, and continuing from where the previous student(s) left off.

After a specified amount of time, call out "switch," and your students get up and move one desk over. Wait a few more minutes and then call "switch" again. Continue this until most of the papers are completed. If a student arrives at a paper that has been completed earlier than the others, that student checks the paper, and then writes comments, suggestions, or praise.

Math: Task rotation is a great way to get kids to complete math worksheets. The excitement of getting up out of one's seat helps the students forget the fact that they are doing routine practice drills.

Story writing: You never can tell where the story will lead!

Drawing and art: This is a playful way to generate some creative—and unlikely—works of art. Each student adds to the design of the preceding students.

Review and closure: After an extended project, I had my 7th graders rotate in small groups to various stations. Each station had a sheet of paper with a different question: "What did you like most about this project?" "What was the most challenging part?" "What would you do differently next time?" It was fabulous to hear and read children's comments, such as "Next time I won't procrastinate so much." Or "The hardest part was staying organized."

Variation: Each student's desk has a single problem or question on it. The students solve each problem as they come to it, bringing their own answers with them as they move around the room. As a student finishes one problem, he or she moves to another desk to begin the next problem. Several extra problems at empty stations will ensure that faster problem-solvers have an unoccupied problem to go to.

■ READERS THEATER

A group of students presents a story to their classmates, with each student within the group reading and dramatizing a role.

Language arts, vocabulary: Here is a variation called "Repetitions." Students recite a statement dramatically two or more times with a different emphasis, tone, etc. For example, a student states, "15 plus 5 equals 20" in the following ways: hesitantly, assertively, defiantly, shyly, arrogantly. In this case, your objective is to foster students' vocabulary related to emotions and personalities. This objective also ties in well with student self-awareness, or to more precisely describe characters in a story.

■ PHYSICALLY ACTIVE, SMALLER GROUP GAMES

These are activities that involve students in groups of two or three.

Gravity Grab

Action, coordination, and lots of eager participation. Students are paired, with one student holding a small ball, scarf, or other object (crumpled balls of paper, often in large supply, work very well). The ball holder stands with arm outstretched, holding the ball with the back of the hand facing up, so that when the grasp is released the ball falls to the floor. The "catcher" places his or her fingers on top of the knuckles of the partner's hand holding the ball. When the "releaser" drops the ball, the catcher attempts to catch it with the one hand before it hits the floor.

Math: Catches, hits, and misses each count a certain number of points. The goal is to make five attempts, and calculate your total score. For primary level catch = 3, hit = 2, and miss = 1. For higher level, catch = ¾, hit = ¼, and miss = ½. You can also figure class means and percent success of dominant versus less dominant hand.

Language arts: "You have just won the gold medal in the Gravity Grab in the Olympics. Prepare a speech for when you are a guest on the evening news tomorrow." Give students ideas for writing—who to thank, how they trained for the event, when they discovered they had this amazing talent and might be in the Olympics.

Standoff

This is a friendly competitive game for two. Students in pairs, preferably of approximately the same height, stand facing each other, arm length apart. Each student has his or her feet together, arms out in front at shoulder height with palms facing the opponent. The object is to get the opponent to lose his or her balance and move his or her feet. You may only make contact with your opponent's palms; you must keep your palms facing your opponent, but you may move your palms forward or back. This is not a game of strength, but of strategy, anticipation, and reflexes.

Self-esteem: This is an esteem boost for kinesthetic and coordinated students, some of whom may not normally be successful with reading, writing, math, and other subjects. Thus, by bringing diverse modalities and experiences into your classroom, you can better discover and validate the talents and interests of all.

Life skills: This game is a metaphor for life, in that it illustrates the importance of strategy versus strength.

Eleven (Finger Math Game)

Students are in groups of three, each holding out one closed fist. On the count of three, each student puts out some number of fingers, from one to five. The goal is for the sum of the group's outstretched fingers to equal eleven. You can't put out the same number twice in a row. Students may not communicate their plans, and groups continue until they reach the sum of eleven. When they do, they of course shake hands and congratulate each other.

Variations are many:

- Change the goal to a sum other than eleven.
- Change the operations—one of the students can be a negative number.
- The three numbers are multiplied.
- Incorporate fractions and multiples—i.e., each finger counts one-half, or each finger counts as two.
- Use both hands.

Instead of aiming for a particular sum, such as eleven, students will get motivating drill practice by calling out the sum (or product), whatever it is. The goal is to see just how fast one can get with the arithmetic operations. The arithmetic will be easier with students in pairs, instead of threes.

■ Physically Active, Larger Group

These are activities that require a larger group or the whole class. Some require moving desks or chairs, or are best for an open area outdoors or in the gym.

Human "Electricity" (Hand-Squeeze Circle)

This is one of the most outstanding whole group team-building games, with excellent applications to math, science, and self-empowerment. Your students form one large circle, holding hands. You initiate an "electric current" in the form of a hand squeeze, which is passed along the circle—students gently squeezes their neighbor's hand when they feel a squeeze from the other neighbor. Using a stopwatch, time how long the "current" takes to go around the entire circle, and record it on whiteboard or a notepad.

Repeat this several times, having the students make predictions about whether they will be able to improve their time and by how much. Generally, a group will improve steadily for five or more trials; then a plateau is reached. Finally, when no more record-breaking times seem likely, tell the class to "focus, take a deep breath, relax, and make this our best time!" It is quite likely that they will break their previous record, illustrating the importance of positive self-belief and focus.

Simulation demonstrating importance of practice: This game, though so simple, does enable students to see that improvement occurs with practice. Point out how one's brain makes learning more and more automatic, and more permanent, with practice.

Math: This human electricity game has many applications to math. For starters, the numbers or data—i.e., the various recorded times—have much more meaning to the students than the abstract numbers of typical math problems. And there is so much one can do with this data . . .

With younger children, practice using a clock, and learning what a second is. Or ask, "How much faster did we just get compared with our first time?" (a subtraction problem). "If we had twice as many people in our group, how long would it take?" (a multiplication problem).

With older children . . . calculate means, compute average individual reaction times (i.e., divide total time by number of individuals in the circle), graph the data (trial number 1, 2, 3, etc., on the X-axis, with seconds on the Y-axis), round-off times to the nearest tenth of a second from hundredths.

I recommend collecting the data one day, and then continue working with the data and doing calculations with it on one or more of the following days. Thus, you spend perhaps 30 minutes playing the game, and generate much more time doing the math.

Science process skills: Test various hypotheses or questions, such as "Would our speed be different in the morning compared with the afternoon?" Or test the hypothesis that reaction times would vary with age; collect data for each grade level in your building.

Trust-Building Play

These are active games that foster laughter and a collaborative spirit.

▸ Hidden-Pass Circle

Your group is in a circle, with one person, the finder, in the center. A small object—a coin or a button—is passed from hand-to-hand around the circle in any direction, with all hands simultaneously pretending to be passing the object. Meanwhile, the finder attempts to locate the object by tapping on the hands of those in the group. The finder gets 5 guesses or 1 minute, whichever comes first. When the finder eventually taps on the correct hand, then that person caught with the object goes to the middle.

Vary the game by including more than one finder, or change the number of objects being passed or the number of guesses. Put several buttons on a large loop of string; each student takes hold of a portion of the loop, and passes the buttons as above. The larger the objects, the more challenging the game!

Cooperation: The Hidden-Pass Circle enhances moods, picks up energy levels, and provides students with a playful, collaborative out-of-seat experience.

Activity reward: "If we get our math worksheets done early, we can play a game."

▸ Connecting Eyes Circle

Students are in a large circle. Each student simply glances around at other individuals in the circle. Whenever two students make eye contact with each other, those two individuals switch places by walking directly across the circle to stand in the spot just occupied by their temporary partner. Children maintain their eye contact until they make it to their new places. And now they are free to search for a new connection. Meanwhile, all other students in the circle are playing at the same time. The result is a random collection of pairs continually crossing and recrossing the circle. The game generally lasts for only a few minutes, but it's a delight.

Communication skills: For younger children, especially, this is a safe way to encourage kids to make eye contact.

Kindergarten: Many of your little ones will love making eye contact with The Teacher! What an empowering, self-esteem building experience!

▸ Circle Role-Play Game

Students are in a circle, with one (or more) students in the middle. Agree in advance on three or four animals to role-play, and what a quick three-person dramatization would be for each animal. The student in the middle of the circle points to someone and calls out one of the animals (e.g., elephant). That student then does an imitation and movements of the animal's head, while the two students on either side act out the big, floppy ears. The three students have only 3 seconds to get it right or one of them goes to the middle.

This is a active, humorous, cooperative venture! Speed up the game by giving students only a split-second to imitate the animal.

Visual and kinesthetic review of concepts: Anything that can be dramatized can be played out with this game. Perhaps you are teaching history—for each historical figure, develop a three-person dramatization that captures some essential facet of that individual's contributions or era.

Vocabulary: Instead of a three-person dramatization, make it just one person. The individual pointed to must quickly dramatize one of the vocabulary words. (This game easily illustrates that teachers can teach an entire lesson to prepare the kids for the game.) Thus, spend 15 or 20 minutes modeling each of the vocabulary words, while students collaboratively develop with you a suitable dramatization. Some examples: "democracy," dramatize voting; "dictatorship," act bossy. This is an outstanding game to teach descriptors of feelings, attitudes, personalities (e.g., tense, ecstatic, philanthropic, nervous, frustrated, relaxed).

Add complexity by increasing the number of actions/words—four or five or maybe ten! Encourage student leadership, decision-making, and team-building skills by giving students the responsibility for developing the dramatization and other rules.

▸ Meet Your Neighbor

This one's a favorite, especially with younger children! Your group is seated in a circle. One person stands in the middle, walks up to any seated individual, and, while shaking hands, says, "I'd like to meet your neighbors." The seated individual introduces his or her neighbors, and then asks, "Who else would you like to meet?" The student in the center replies, for example, "I'd like to meet everyone wearing blue." At which point everyone with blue in their clothes must leave their seat and find a different, nonadjacent one, while the person in the center rushes to find a seat. Whoever is left in the center then continues the game as above. Lots of panicky rushing for seats, and lots of laughter.

Be sure to encourage students to come up with a wide spectrum of requests; you can create a menu of possibilities on the whiteboard for reference. More interesting requests relate to individual interests and life experiences, rather than physical attributes and type of clothing.

Learning names, team building, self-awareness, play: Need we say more?

Review of concepts: Distribute to each student a card with a word, picture, or number on it. Students "become" their card. Thus, you might distribute cards having numbers on them. The student in the middle might state, "I'd like to meet an even number," or "I'd like to meet a multiple of 5." Each student whose card matches that stated attribute gets up to find another chair. After two or three rounds, call "pass," and each student passes his or her card one person to the right. This ensures that students get plenty of review with a number of concepts.

Chapter 11
Simple, Familiar, and Versatile Tools

This is a collection of mostly familiar tools that have enormous versatility.

■ LISTING

For this highly versatile tool, students are given the task of listing words (or phrases) that describe or relate to any stated concept.

Listing and brainstorming—which follow—are closely related. As used here, listing is a simple recall of attributes, associations, or observations. Brainstorming tasks involve a more complex question or problem. For example:

> "List all of the countries you can think of."
> "Brainstorm the solutions to world poverty."

The power of listing lies in its open-ended, nonthreatening nature and its briefness. Students perceive the task as inviting, rather painless, and personally meaningful. Students take ownership of this task because the words generated are their own. And significantly, you save time and paper because there is no need to prepare worksheets.

Reading comprehension: "List attributes of Abraham Lincoln, based upon our readings and discussion."

Writing: By creating and posting lists of adjectives, synonyms for overused words, etc, students will have a word bank to access for their writing.

Social studies: "List characteristics of an ideal world." "List the parts of a government." "List all the things that taxes pay for."

Science: "List the sources of error in the experiment. List the variables." "List all they types of animals you can think of."

Self-awareness, vocabulary: "List words that describe people." "List twenty-five words that describe yourself." "List feelings that you have toward summer; toward winter."

Values, discussion: "List five things that are worth more than money. Explain why. Which two of the five are the most valuable?"

Vocabulary, idea production: "List twenty different colors." "List all flavors of ice cream." "List all one-syllable words ending in the letter B." "List thirty words that could describe the weather."

Follow-up Learning from Lists

These lists are outstanding lesson starters. Some ideas . . . Alphabetize the list; sort or classify by number of syllables. Focus on synonyms, related words, and vocabulary development. Use the lists to lead in to poetry or creative writing; students' lists become a word bank from which they readily find the words they want. Follow up with student sharing and discussion. Use the activity as a vehicle for motivating students to observe closely.

Example #1: "List fifty words that come to mind when you think about a pizza." Students' lists would likely encompass physical attributes of pizza, their experiences, and their attitudes. (Carefully choose your examples—in this case, if some of your students have not ever eaten a pizza, you're better off with a different item, or a choice of items.)

As follow-up to this pizza example, you may proceed to classifying (words grouped by sense), to spelling and the use of a dictionary, to creative writing (write a story about the best pizza in the world), to nutrition, or to team building skills (how can we design one pizza that will satisfy the entire class).

Example #2: "List all the words that come to mind when you think of Dr. Seuss." Lead in to a discussion comparing Dr. Seuss with other authors the children like.

Example #3 (Social studies and math): Students have 3 minutes to list places anywhere in the world. Then they use maps and globes to measure the distances to those places. As an extension, students use a travel Web site, e.g., Travelocity, to find airfares from their home to and the nearest airport at that place. Award an imaginary prize to the student who finds the most expensive airfare!

Example #4: "List all inventions that you can see from where you are seated, e.g., glass, windows, doorknob, paint, language."

As a follow-up, students can research and report on one of these inventions. Most students will be amazed at the length of their list, at the vast number of ways in which humans have made changes to their environment.

Example #5: Historical ingredients: Prior to learning about a particular region's history, students first brainstorm a hypothetical list of possible events and resources that might be significant to that area's history. The list might include items such as war, oil, timber, poverty, political leaders, etc.

Next have them put the items in what they believe is a possible chronological order according to the sequence that each of the items might appear in a history textbook. I used this activity successfully with an Alaska state history course—the free-flow of student ideas and sharing helped initiate student thinking and questioning prior to the presentation of factual information. It enabled students to ponder a framework for the history they were about to learn.

Listing—Simple, Quick, Versatile, and Effective

In summary, listing is an exceedingly powerful tool to add to your repertoire, at least in part because it is so versatile and takes such minimal preparation. The divergent nature encourages students to find personal meaning and enjoyment. Use it freely at a number of points in your lesson or unit—motivational lead-in as well as review and closure. Just be sure to use it!

■ BRAINSTORMING

Although brainstorming is often thought of as a creative problem-solving technique, its power and versatility go far beyond that.

The basic technique is as follows: Students in cooperative groups are given a specific question or problem, and are to generate many responses in a short amount of time.

Encourage students to respond freely, with all reasonable responses being accepted without judging them. Small-group work generally yields the most favorable results, because it facilitates active participation from a greater number of students of all ability levels and interests.

A sampling of items to brainstorm:

> things made from plastic . . . political figures . . . careers . . . beginning letters and colors . . . words with double letters . . . possible themes for a short story . . . questions to ask a salesman before you buy a skateboard . . . ways to solve a particular problem . . . resources for information on traveling in Peru . . . types of animals . . . cities in the United States . . . hobbies . . . fairy tale characters . . .

Or try some "what if" brainstorms: What if snow were green? What if there were no Saturday?

Suggestions for effective brainstorming: Initially, seek quantity, variety, and originality of ideas. You can proceed further with more detail, elaboration, and evaluation of those ideas. Or select particular responses for further discussion or writing—e.g., the realistic ones, or the creative ones.

Set a time limit, usually only 2 to 5 minutes. Accept all responses without judgment or evaluation. Encourage quantity of responses and piggybacking of one student's ideas upon another's. Be sure each group has at least one recorder to write down everyone's ideas.

Ownership of learning: You can have the students brainstorm a list of what they might brainstorm! Then, have the students choose from that list to brainstorm again!

Word Associations Brainstorm

Example: "Brainstorm all the ideas, words, and feelings that come to mind when you think of the word 'winter.'" This can be a springboard to writing, or to an assigned reading, or to learning about seasons.

Improvements Brainstorm

This brainstorming version is directed toward improving a task, idea, or anything else. These can be related readily to the learner's world, and invite both creative and critical thinking. Your emphasis can be serious and content-related, or humorous and creative. Some examples for students to brainstorm:

Science and technology: "Think how to improve a computer" (or clothes, or an apple).

Study skills: "Brainstorm ways to do better in school"

P.E.: "Brainstorm ways to improve our basketball team."

Global issues, social studies: "How can we enhance global cooperation?" "How can we reduce air pollution?"

The final output can be class discussion, individual essays, research, or artistic representations of the improved product (drawings or three-dimensional structures, for example).

Creative Brainstorms

Since all brainstorming is essentially a creative act, the following two types of brainstorms are labeled "creative" more as an arbitrary convenience than anything else.

Answer-to-question: Given an answer, the objective is to generate questions. For example: "The answer is 'A tree in the forest.'"

Suitable questions might include "What do woodpeckers build their nests in?" "What do you hide behind if a bear is chasing you?" "What can you make paper from?"

Alternate uses: Given the name of an item, students are given 2 minutes to write down as many uses as possible associated with the word.

"What uses are there for a block of wood?" Possible answers include . . . paperweight, use it for carving, door jamb, firewood, make wood chips for your garden, etc.

Positive, Interesting, and Negative (PIN)

Noted thinking-skills author Edward de Bono (1985) asks, "What if food were in pills?" Students first brainstorm three lists—the positive effects, the interesting effects, and the negative effects. Give kids perhaps 1 to 2 minutes for each list. Learners then convert each of the negatives into a positive. For example, if "eating would be boring" was listed under negative, then converting that to a positive might be to have artistic patterns on the pills, or to flavor each of them differently. At the content level, these "what if" questions can be readily incorporated into the beginning or end of lessons to generate a synthesis or application of the unit's concepts.

Biology: "Do a PIN for Insects." This would be a useful synthesis for a biology unit on insects. It reinforces students' knowledge of insects as both beneficial and harmful to our well-being. You can do the same for bacteria.

Language arts: The PIN lists generated by cooperative learning groups are readily expanded into individual student essays. The brainstormed lists provide an idea bank that quickly engages students. Otherwise, many students just sit there—"I don't know what to write," they complain.

Self-awareness, values, sharing: Do a PIN on such topics as winter, family, friends, life, school.

■ Task Series Technique (TST)

With this simple technique, students perform a prescribed series of steps in a set of instructions. For example, in the *"listen-think-do"* version, students first listen to a list of instructions, then think about or visualize the list, and finally perform the sequence.

A simple playful version might be as follows: "Listen carefully to the following set of directions, but don't do anything yet. After I give you the directions, I am going to ask you to follow them. First, just listen: I'd like you to stand, turn in a circle, touch your toes, tap your pencil on your desk, and then sit down. OK, now think through each of the steps. [Teacher waits a few moments.] OK, now do it."

Although the example above may lead you to believe this is merely a motivating filler, in actuality the technique is widely applicable. The TST enables you to train students to handle a series of tasks presented at one time, thus cutting down on the transition times that occur when you must get their attention after each individual task during a period. You can get your students accustomed to taking the daily lessons and homework assignments orally, thus cutting down on the number of instructions that must be written on the whiteboard. At the least, both you and your students now know that they *can* remember three or four directions—because while playing this "game" they demonstrate that very ability.

Use the TST in any one of its many forms:

> *Listen-think-do:* This is the example given above.
> *Listen-share-do:* Students share in small groups to verify with their neighbors that they each heard the information accurately.
> *Listen-write-share-do:* Students take notes on the presented information to insure more accurate retention. Outstanding for secondary students.
> *Listen-draw-share:* Ideal for primary students. For example: "Draw a house; put a tree next to the house, and a bird in the tree."
> *Observe-write-share:* Students observe an object, or a film, take notes on their observations, then share their notes with a partner to verify areas of agreement and to identify discrepancies among their observations.

The TST is enormously useful and flexible for developing listening skills, retention, and visualizing skills. Students can be grouped cooperatively for the task, or one student can volunteer while others observe and coach him. As students develop their skills, the sequence can be made progressively longer.

What a stupendous opportunity to train students to listen to the entire set of instructions first, rather than acting on the first bit of information and missing entirely the instructions that follow.

■ Stems and Completions

Students are presented with a part of a sentence, a story, a poem, or a biography—and their task is to complete it.

Stems provide enough structure and focus to prompt the student in the right direction, yet are open-ended enough to encourage ample thinking, individuality and creativity.

Consider using stems in the following ways:

> *To start a lesson:* Generate student participation and connecting of the lesson to students' own lives.
>
> *To pre-test informally:* Determine in advance what students may already know (correctly or incorrectly) about an upcoming unit.
>
> *To reinforce learning:* Enable students to integrate newly learned concepts into their own cognitive framework. This facilitates ownership of learning and retention.

Sentence Stems

In a sentence stem, you provide the first part of the sentence, and students finish it.

Academic content, writing:

> "Five things about the United States are . . ."
> "Winter is . . ."
> "If my best friend got cancer . . ."
> "My favorite part of _____ is _____."
> "I was surprised that I . . ."
> "I was pleased that I . . ."

Self-awareness and goal setting:

> "Something I want to accomplish this year is . . ."
> "I'd like to be . . ."
> "In this class, I'd most like . . ."
> "The next problem I run into, I will . . ."
> "I am happiest (proudest, saddest, angriest) when . . ."
> "Two things I like about myself are . . ."
> "If I could change one thing about myself (my family, my classroom, our planet, technology, politics), it would be . . ."
> "I am willing to trust . . ."
> "I wonder . . ."

Random stems: Have students generate their own sentence stems. Collect the stems, and redistribute them randomly. Each student then completes the stem he or she receives.

Seed stems: Have students in cooperative groups brainstorm a list of stems; each child is then asked to write a story generated from a stem ("seed") of his or her choosing.

Story Predictions and Completions

Prior to an assigned reading—a novel, biography, or news article—describe for the class two or more clues to the nature of the reading. Students, either in groups or individually, then create their own imagined plots or outcomes, to be shared aloud with the class.

Example: One teacher tried this strategy before introducing her class to *The Lord of the Flies*. She wrote three clues on the board—airplane crash, fifteen boys under the age of 14, and tropical island.

Motivation, reading comprehension: This lead-in may intrigue students enough to pursue their assigned readings. As a playful closure, read back the students' creative versions after they have read the entire story.

▸ Creative Math Completions

These are math word problems with some or all of the parts left blank. What a creative open-ended opportunity for students to generate and then solve their own problems! Aha, you say, another trick where kids will think they're playing. Precisely.

> "Andrew has _____ apples, and gave _____ away to his friends. He now has _____ left."
>
> "Fortunately, the _____ were on sale for _____ percent off. Unfortunately, since I only had _____ dollars left, I could only buy _____ of them. I can't wait to _____ when I get home with them."

■ SEARCH TASKS AND SCAVENGER HUNTS

Search tasks involve the students in locating ideas, information, or resources. Commonly referred to as scavenger hunts, search tasks have a motivational and instructional versatility that warrants their use in nearly any classroom.

Letter sounds, spelling, shapes: "Find things in the room that begin with the letter 'm.' Find something that ends in the letter 'd.'" "Find things in the room that are two syllables." "Find pictures in these magazines that contain circles, squares, triangles."

Literature: "Find the lines in the poem that are a metaphorical comparison to a plant; reflect on the poet's attitude toward winter."

Grammar: Take a popular song, and find all the nouns, adjectives, etc.

Study skills, life skills: "Find the page numbers in the encyclopedia for the following: the population of Kansas, where iron ore is mined, when Mozart was born." "Find the heading in the Yellow Pages for locating each of the following: a store that sells fishing tackle, an Italian restaurant, a place to buy wood to build a fence, the price of a fish tank."

Social studies: Students search newspapers for . . . examples of graphic organizers, one article on politics, one article on another country.

Math: "Find things in the room that have a right angle, an acute angle, an obtuse angle." "Find objects that are 1 meter long, 5 cm long, 1 mm long." "Find objects that are approximately 10 sq. cm, 50 sq. cm, 100 sq. inches."

Vocabulary, values and awareness, outdoor field trips, and assorted others: "Find things that are fuzzy, beautiful, something you wish you were, something surprising, something to share with a friend." "Find something rotund, something detrimental, something omnivorous."

Geography: One student writes down the name of a natural or political geographic feature. Other students search for the feature.

Primary grades, learning shapes: Find something square . . . round . . . spherical.

Environment: Find something . . . biodegradable . . . made from fossil fuels . . . made from plants . . . made from animals.

Music: Create a musical hunt—students identify elements in a musical recording, such as changes in tempo, or the presence of particular instruments. "Listen for as many different musical instruments as you can." "Find three different moods in this piece of music."

Ice-breaking, team-building: Create a people scavenger hunt with items such as the following: "Find someone who is taller than you . . . has blue eyes . . . collects baseball cards . . . etc."

Thinking skills, focusing: The "media search" is a simple yet powerful means for focusing students on a film or presentation. Prior to watching a film on a particular topic, students brainstorm anything they know or expect to see related to the film. During the film, the students check off each item on their list as they observe it in the film.

For younger children, or to facilitate visual/spatial modalities, the list can be pictures rather than words. Or try textures for kinesthetic/tactile lessons. For auditory modalities, the list can be sounds or music instead of words.

Errors Search

Searching for errors is often motivating to students. You can do this playfully as well as with authentic resources.

▸ Playful Error Searches

Present the students with an essay, a worksheet, or a scientific experiment in which there are intentional errors planted. As students search excitedly for errors, they are developing and practicing the concepts, as well as their critical thinking skills. Children can develop their own error searches—one student purposely plants errors for other students to find.

Writing: This is a motivating, low-risk way to let children practice their editing skills. One fun version is to take out all punctuation from a paragraph, and purposely read it with pauses and inflections in all the wrong places. Then give the paragraph to students, who need to add the punctuation. Or try too much punctuation: "Last year my family, and I went. On a trip to, California we had a. Great time."

Science: Present a scientific experiment with errors in the method. Here is a primary grades example: To test whether seeds need light to germinate, place five seeds on a countertop and check them the next day. The errors students might notice include "But, they can't germinate if there's no water," or "The seeds need more than one day to sprout." The teacher responds, "Well, how can we fix this experiment?"

▸ Authentic Error Searches

Students search for errors in data or resources of real-world relevance. Your goal is to develop in children the ability to critically assess the quality of the data and opinions—expert and otherwise—that flood our society in this information age. Help kids to see that there is an enormous amount of information available, but not all of it is high quality.

Social studies: "What errors (or inaccurate assumptions) are being made by the author of this editorial?" "Which of these errors might be intentional?"

Science: "What are the sources of error in this data?" "What changes in the design of the investigation would eliminate some of those errors?"

Peer checking: After faster learners complete their assignments, they can search for errors, or areas that can be improved, in their peers' work.

■ CLASSIFYING AND SEQUENCING TASKS

Here is a broad spectrum of tools for almost any learning environment. One of our brain's most significant tasks throughout life is the discovery of patterns. We do this by sorting or ordering an enormous diversity of sensory experiences and mental constructs. The tools here help students practice inductive thinking, i.e., going from the parts to the whole.

Two basic types of sorting tasks are groupings and sequences:

> Groupings have an attribute in common, but there is no particular order.
> Sequences have a logical order, such as one-syllable, then two, and so on.

Students can group or sequence virtually anything—words, objects, people, opinions, experiences, abstract symbols, or artwork.

Important note: You can present these to children with enthusiasm and wonder, and the kids respond with the same attitudes. If you present these as bland, rote worksheet-like drills, you can be sure the result will be equally unimpressive. The key point is this—it's all in the "packaging." Each tool, including these, take on an energy according to the energy you invest in them.

Classifying or Grouping Tasks

Social studies: Start with a list of words and have students sort (i.e., classify) the words into groups according to either your criteria or students' criteria. Students can then label each group or list the groups' attributes.

"Here are three words sharing something in common: Rome, London, and Paris."

With the previous example, one correct answer would be "cities in Europe." You can play around with even one example such as this one by extending it in a number of ways. And by doing so, you reinforce thinking and learning.

Name the group: "Name the group as exactly as possible by identifying all the attributes that the items have in common." (In the example, one could narrow it down from "European cities" to "Western European cities.")

Add to the group—examples and non-examples: "Add more items to the group, and create another list which does not belong in this group."

Here are a couple of examples with classifying and thinking skills.

For each cluster of words, name or describe the category:

> Group #1: Toaster, cat, bowl
> Group #2: Shark, whale, hermit crab, jellyfish

Name the group: The first group can be "living and non-living things," or "living and non-living things found in a house," or "things that you can put food in." How about "things that fall when you drop them"? You really can have fun with these!

If you are teaching life science, you can name the second group "animals that live in water," or more precisely "animals that live in salt water."

Delete one or more to change the name of the group: If you delete hermit crab, you would have "saltwater animals without shells." If you delete jellyfish, you might have "saltwater animals that don't sting." If you delete whale and shark, you might get "saltwater invertebrates." You can also add to the group so the name doesn't change, or add to the group so the name *does* change.

Have students create and change the groupings, with their peers trying to pick up enough of a pattern to be able to name the group. It is worth noting that you can generate these mini-lessons quickly with minimal planning. Thus, if the student engagement is there, or you want to reinforce particular skills or concepts, extend the lesson. Otherwise, move on to something else. The tool gives you ample flexibility to be in the moment with the kids.

Primary grades, and math patterns: Use manipulatives, such as pattern blocks, nuts and bolts, leaves. Have the kids create groups, and their classmates try and figure out the key attributes, or other items to add to the groups.

Teaching or reviewing attributes of a concept: When students can give examples of a concept, and state the attributes of that concept, then clearly they have a solid grasp of the concept.

Creative and critical thinking: You can be playful and creative, as well as quite challenging and abstract. It's a quick way to foster the skills of comparing or classifying, especially if students are manipulating hands-on materials rather than words.

Riddles or problems: "If a store sells one for 1 dollar, ten for 2 dollars, and 100 for 3 dollars, what might they be selling?" (One correct answer: The numbers you tack next to your front door to mark your street address.)

"My friend is allergic to grapefruit, lemon, and tangerines. What else is this person likely to be allergic to, and why?"

These are enormously flexible tools with minimal prep time for you.

Sequencing Tasks

Challenging example: "These three words are in a logical sequence: doll, apple, cities. Which of these could be next? Tree, hamburger, iodine, skiing."

Ask students what criterion or rule they used (size of object, alphabetical order, etc.).

[Answer: In the challenging example, it is the number of vowels that increases by one in each consecutive word, so iodine would be next. Of course, you might come up with another equally consistent rule for the sequence.]

"Put the following in order: hamburger, grass, cow." [Answer: grass, cow, hamburger—first you need the grass to feed the cow in order to get the hamburger.]

Math, patterns: Using any type of object or symbol, students create an extended pattern. Other children try to guess what could be added next. Have students create challenging patterns for you to solve—they love it when the teacher doesn't have the answer!

■ Serial Response Games

These are tools in which students respond one at a time in sequence as they complete a series. The series could be of the convergent type, with one right answer, such as counting by twos, reciting the alphabet, or spelling a word.

Divergent types are open-ended, with many correct responses. A simple sharing circle is an example of this type—students one-by-one could be sharing one thing they learned in their social studies unit, or sharing their thoughts and feelings at the end of the day. There are endless variations within each type and interesting ways to combine different types.

Serial response games are marvelous for enhancing active participation, motivation, and cooperation.

Quick review: These games are so simple and quick, you can use those spare moments productively (e.g., at the end of the day waiting for the bell).

Spelling Circle

This is a simple, quick version of a serial response game. Students are grouped in small circles of, say, four to ten individuals. One student starts with one of the spelling words, with each student around the circle in turn saying one letter in sequence until the entire word is spelled. Spelling circles facilitate visualizing the spelled word without being able to see it. You can readily play this game with students in pairs as well.

Motivation: Many children love this game; they think they're playing. (They *are* playing. They're also learning.) Encourage them to "beat your best time" by seeing how fast they can spell the words around the circle.

Poor spellers: Encourage these students to have their printed list of words in front of them to look at if they get stuck. This reduces errors, makes the task less intimidating, and further reinforces learning.

Alphabet circle version for early primary: Instead of spelling a word, just practice the alphabet. You can go from A to Z, or start at any letter and go to any other letter. Let the first student pick the starting and ending letters.

Nim and Counting-Circles

Nim and its many variations can be motivating practice for counting, reviewing fractions, learning the alphabet, spelling, and problem-solving. (Where did the name "Nim" come from, you ask? Please let me know.)

Students are in a small circle of two to twelve children—actually, the exact number is not important, and neither is the circle! One person starts counting, beginning with the number one. That first person, and each successive person around the circle, may count off either one, two, or three numbers at a time. Then the person to the right has a turn to count off one, two, or three numbers, beginning where the last person left off. For example: "One-two," "three," "four-five-six," etc. As the numbers are counted around the circle, eventually one person counts "fifteen, and this person sits and is out. The game continues till only one person is left.

Reinforce counting or fractions: There are many variations possible. For example, you can count by ones, with each child having the option to say one, two, or three numbers. Or start at eight, counting backwards to three, reciting by halves. As you can see, there is an enormous number of variations. Or start at 7, count backwards into negative integers, and the person who says minus 5 is out.

You can change any of four things to vary the game's focus or difficulty: (1) the starting point, (2) the ending point, (3) the interval (for example, count by twos or threes), and (4) the individual's options (for example, can count just one number, or up to three numbers).

Problem-solving, higher-level math: Same Nim game, but with only two players. The main objective now is for students to problem-solve how to always be assured of winning the game—i.e., getting the other person to say the end number—when playing in groups of two. Make it more concrete by playing with a pile of fifteen coins or pencils, rather than playing verbally.

In the example with the option of saying three numbers, you can always win if you end your turn on two, then six, then ten, then fourteen. (Don't take my word for it. See for yourself.)

Primary version: Place five objects in a pile. One child may pick one or two objects. Then the opponent may pick one or two objects. The last person to pick an object wins. As the children figure out a strategy, increase the level of difficulty by starting with six objects, then seven, etc.

Simultaneous Modalities Circle

In this variation, you include additional movements or sounds, in addition to the verbal responses. There are innumerable variations; here is one basic version called "fizz-buzz."

Students are in a circle, either standing or seated. Beginning at one point in the circle, each student in turn counts by ones. When any student is at a multiple of three, the student says "fizz" instead of the number. For multiples of five, the student says "buzz." And for multiples of both three and five, the student says "fizz buzz." Therefore, the counting would go like this: one-two-fizz-four-buzz-fizz-seven-eight-fizz-buzz-eleven-fizz-thirteen-fourteen-fizzbuzz.

Competitive version: Students who make an error are eliminated from the competition, but may still participate. The last person remaining is the winner.

Cooperative version: Set speed and accuracy goals for the whole group. For example, try to make it all the way around the circle in less than 2 minutes or with no more than two errors.

Spelling: Combine fizz-buzz with the spelling circle—each time the letter is a vowel, students clap their hands while saying the letter.

You can change any of three things to vary the game's focus or difficulty: (1) the signal, (2) the counting interval, or (3) the key attribute. For example, in the standard version the signals are fizz and buzz, you are counting by ones, and the key attributes are multiples of three and five. You can also change the signal to snapping of fingers, counting by twos, with the key attribute (for the finger snapping) being multiples of ten. The combinations are infinite—which means the kids can easily generate their own versions.

Important idea . . . when the kids can do something themselves, you shouldn't have to! Nor should you want to!

Name Circle

This is an excellent icebreaker, enabling group members to readily learn each other's names. Extensions of the name circle can be used for team building and fun.

Students form circles of up to ten or twenty. Most teachers will want to split their class into two or three groups. One person begins by saying his or her name; the person on the left (or right) then says his or her name followed by the first person's name. The next person in line says his or her name, then the second person's, followed by the first person's name. This continues along the circle, the chain of names becoming longer and longer.

Eventually, one person will have trouble remembering so many names. At this point, go back to the first person and start the name chain from the beginning, but this time in the opposite direction.

Continue until the group can make it all around the circle with no (or very few) mistakes. Finally, scramble the circle and ask for a couple volunteers to name everyone around the new circle.

For variations, instead of first names, use last names. Or have students come up with a word (e.g., an animal name or an interest) to associate with their name, such as "Basketball Aimee."

Concept/Skill Sequence Circle

Any information that has a sequence can be raw material for this serial response game. Try stating important historical events in chronological order, or listing the steps in a complex process (e.g., a wood shop project or the sequence of steps in digestion).

Primary: Think of the procedures that your children need to memorize when they arrive at school in the morning, or for cleanup, or for rainy day recess. Younger children can do a choral response, rather than just one student at a time.

Before/After Sequence Game

Children are seated in a small circle. One student walks around the circle, randomly choosing one seated child and saying a number (or letter, event in a story, or other item in a series). The child on the right gives the next item in the series, while the student on the left gives the preceding item. This can be a quick, playful review for a variety of lesson objectives.

Math: Vary the intervals between numbers. You can have the series go by halves, tenths, fives, tens, hundreds, or geometric progressions. Review the series of place values from ones to thousands, or for higher grades, from thousandths to billions. To review rounding off, have the student on the right round to hundreds and the student on the left round to tens.

Language arts: Reinforce alphabetizing. Practice the sequence of events in a story's plot, or the steps in writing a research paper.

Social studies: Review a series of historical events, or the order of presidents.

Middle school science: The series can be elements of the periodic chart, electron configurations, the kingdom-phylum-class sequence, or steps in a complex procedure.

■ PAIRING GAMES

Pairing games provide quick practice and review. Students are in pairs; one person calls out the one-word question, while the partner calls out the matching answer. Several versions include the following.

Math: For Doubling, one student calls out a number, and the second student must double it. How about trying some variations on the doubling game: halving or quartering or quadrupling. For Sums, one student calls out a number, and the partner must call out a second number which when added to the first, totals to a specified sum. Example: If the sum is 100, the first student calls out 53 and the second student must call out 47.

Geography: How about trying the following? Cities—states, countries—continents.

Language: Word—part of speech, word—synonym or antonym.

Classification and categories: One student calls out an object or category, and the partner names the category. Examples: "Salmon—fish," "rabbit—mammal," etc.

In the "types" version, one partner calls out "a _____ is a type of," and the second student calls out the answer. Example: "Democracy is a type of"—"government."

Creative thinking: The first student gives an "answer," and a partner generates the "question." For example, "Cabbage"—"What vegetable has two Bs in it?"

In limited response pairing, student responses are confined to a specific set, such as true/false, fact/opinion, vertebrate/invertebrate, whole number/fraction, etc. For example, types of information are called out, and the answer must be either "Encyclopedia" or "Dictionary," depending upon which source would provide that information.

Responses can be given with hand signals instead of verbally, and this lends itself well to whole-group choral responses. This whole-group technique is then useful for monitoring the students' learning during a quick practice session.

In open-ended response pairings, students are able to generate a wider range of answers on their own. For example, for the word "whale," acceptable responses might include large, marine mammal, intelligent.

Equivalent fractions: One student calls out a fraction, and the partner calls out an equivalent.

Rounding off: One student calls out a number, and the place to be rounded to. The second student rounds the given number to that place.

■ TASK LISTS/TO-DO LISTS

Get students in the habit of maintaining lists of what they need to do. Help them to organize and prioritize these lists. Young children can easily make their lists by drawing pictures or symbols.

Student responsibility: When students create their own task lists (with the teacher's facilitation, of course), there is likely to be more cognitive processing, better ownership, and retention.

Social studies: "You have just been elected president of the United States. Create a 'to-do list.' Prioritize it." (This is also an example of a scenario.)

Project-based learning: "Brainstorm all the things you need to do to complete your project. Put these steps in order. Write a date for when you will work on that step."

Middle school literature: "You are a great author, and you want to write a novel. Make a list of everything you would want to consider in planning your story."

■ DISCOVERIES

Help students to actively notice more—whether it be hidden or novel, a pattern or connection. You do this by exposing students to any experience—literature, film, life experiences, science investigations, maps—and then asking them to search for anything new to them.

Language arts: After students have experienced any piece of literature, ask "What do you notice?"

Maps: I had my students make a list of ten discoveries, anything at all that they didn't know beforehand. It might be that the Yukon River is in Alaska or that Rhode Island is really small or discovering on a map for the first time one's place of birth.

Science: After collecting data during any investigation, ask "What do you notice about the data? What do you think looking at our results? What doesn't the data tell you? Which pieces of data, if any, seem to be errors, or out of place?"

Social studies, science: Have students examine any collection of data—population data, a tide chart, opinion survey data—and ask them to just find patterns, ask questions, discover hypotheses.

Math: Encourage students to see patterns in numbers. For example, in the following addition problem, $8 + 4 + 9 + 1 + 2$, you may notice that you can group the $8 + 2$ and the $9 + 1$.

Field trips: Have students make a couple of discoveries. It has to be something most people wouldn't notice, and something that is interesting or unusual in some way.

■ TIME LINES

Time lines facilitate sequential organization of content and ideas, and can be adapted to a variety of objectives—self-awareness, goal-setting, problem-solving, creative writing, or discussion. Apply them not only to an individual's life, but also to the "lives" of the following:

Characters from novels, or from history. A country. A technology (e.g., TV). A way of life (e.g., farming). A particular political system, such as democracy or communism.

Language arts, writing: Students use their time line as a sequential organizer for generating a biographical or autobiographical essay.

Sequence the day: Primary students make a timeline showing what they do from when they arise in the morning, till nighttime.

Branching Time Lines

These are time lines with additional branches heading off into the future. For example, "Draw a branch that represents what you see happening if you go to college, draw another branch if you win a million dollars, and draw a third branch reflecting what you believe is most likely." Students not only list past events/experiences (especially positive ones), but also create an imagined positive future for themselves.

Stories: After students are partway through a short story or novel, they create branches leading to alternative conjectures for where the story will lead.

Middle school social studies: "Create a 'life tree' for your own life, with a branch for each of the following:

> 1. The future is a simple continuation of the present, no drastic changes.
> 2. Global warming creates enormous climate change, leading to worldwide shifts in climate. The results include severe droughts, sshortages of food, political and economic instability of nations, and increased crime and increased global tensions leading to more frequent wars.
> 3. Countries throughout the world unselfishly begin to move toward a more global consciousness as leaders resolve to work together to achieve global peace, prosperity, and environmental health.

You may choose to be realistic or creative, optimistic or pessimistic. Be sure to focus on your own life within each of the three contexts."

■ COMPARE/CONTRAST

Take advantage of the versatility and power of compare/contrast. You can promote content learning, thinking skills, creativity, self-awareness, or values. The task is straightforward—students are to list similarities and differences for a pair of words or objects.

Thinking skills, self-awareness, and values: Even the simplest comparisons of concepts we take for granted can yield illuminating insights and fascinating open-ended discussion. Some comparisons to explore include the following:

> Sleep/awake
> Thinking/daydreaming
> The future/the past
> Brilliant/crazy
> Brave/foolish
> Work/play
> To love/to like
> Optimistic/naïve
> School/life

Content learning: Compare/contrast reinforces concept acquisition by prompting an analysis of a concept's critical attributes. Try the following:

> Democracy/dictatorship
> Nouns/verbs
> Animal/plant
> Poetry/prose

Creativity and metaphorical associations: Pick a pair of words that are very dissimilar—the crazier the better! You will no doubt have at least a few learners who cherish this opportunity to generate connections that are illogical, fantastic, poetic, and free. Some possible word pairs include the following:

> Moon/green cheese
> Laughter/clouds
> Peace/beauty

Similarities version: Have students list only the ways in which the two items are similar. Encourage answers that go beyond the obvious, delve into metaphor, or uncover interrelationships.

■ Deductive Logic

There are many variations of these. They afford students an opportunity to enjoy persevering, to practice logical/analytical skills.

Try this one: "You have just landed on a strange planet. On the planet are two types of people. There are liars, who always lie, and truth-tellers, who always tell the truth. You can ask one person you meet only one question to determine what that person is. What question will you ask?"

Further ideas . . .

Problem-solving skills and metacognition: Have students share with classmates the thinking strategies that helped them solve the problem. This helps students become more cognizant of their thinking skills, which in turn helps them be better thinkers.

Enrichment: Have advanced students develop their own problems by starting with a solution, and then working backwards providing just enough clues for the answer to be found.

Math: Although many of these logic puzzles are word problems, students are generally able to solve them more easily by drawing pictures of the problem or organizing the data into a chart or grid. Both methods are important math skills.

■ The Randomization Technique

Add a bit of randomness to a lesson. For example, have students randomly pick their particular assigned math problems from a box filled with a mix of choices.

Simple, Familiar, and Versatile Tools 107

The elements of chance, variety, and play stimulate motivation and ownership of the assignment. Think about it—don't we all get excited to open fortune cookies!

Here's an example I used with my 7th graders: I flipped a coin, and lost. It meant I had to eat an entire school lunch. Half a dozen kids observed me intently to make sure I ate every pea. I said, "This isn't bad." They said, "Yeah, sure." I was laughing so hard, it was difficult to eat.

P.S. They love when you lose graciously, or when you make a mistake and laugh at yourself. One of the best strategies, once you have the rapport and the sense of community, is for your students to have many, many experiences of helping you when you misplace your glasses, or when you misspell a word, or when they beat you at chess. So, please . . . it's good for you to be competent; and it's even better for them to experience the real you—confident, imperfect, organized (usually!), humble, willing to learn, and eager to laugh.

Chapter 12
Art, Drama, Music, and the Senses

Regardless of age, whether 6 years old or 18, most students become more actively involved when the experience is hands-on, sensory, or physically active. Make it a habit to think first of activities that truly engage children. You can usually find ways to creatively infuse the learning outcomes that you need to teach within these child-centered activities. This reverse planning becomes increasingly natural and efficient for you the more you do it.

■ ARTISTIC EXPRESSION AND DRAWING

The following ideas are catalysts to prompt your own talents and creativity, and starting points for connecting to your own students and learning outcomes.

Math Art

Give the kids colored construction paper, ribbons, string, magazine photos, or other materials. Specify sizes, shapes, and lengths that the children must incorporate to create their artwork. You can estimate and measure the lengths, perimeters, and areas. Students can lay their shapes on graph paper and count squares to confirm surface areas. Estimate also the perimeter of each shape, then lay a string along the edges and measure the string. You can do this measuring to get practice with inches, fractions of an inch, centimeters, and millimeters.

Doodle Art

Develop borders for title pages. Give awards for best doodling. Use calligraphy pens. Many students love to doodle—encourage them, give them ideas.

Primary/Patterns: Doodling provides relaxing practice for reinforcing the design and appreciation of patterns and symmetry. Teacher: "Today's doodle rule is that your doodles have to include squares, stars, and a repeating pattern. You have exactly 10 minutes."

On occasion, begin with the things students enjoy—e.g., doodling—and then design academic learning outcomes from these activities. I call this "reverse planning."

Concept Drawings

Students draw on single sheets of paper to communicate an assigned concept, theme, or person.

▸ Autobiographical Drawings

Students very much enjoy this! The children each draw a picture that illustrates something about their lives. You can provide a list of prompts for what to include—e.g., individuals in your family, interests and hobbies, or places and things you love.

The drawings can be quick stick figures, or more detailed. It *is* necessary that students have fun with this; it is *not* at all necessary that students have drawing talent. The pictures are then shared as students introduce their pictures and themselves to their classmates. For example, each student shows his or her picture to a classmate, who will try and guess what the other person's picture is communicating. Or students each post pictures on the wall, and everyone tries to guess whose picture is whose.

Early in the school year: This is a pleasant, non-threatening activity that allows children to get to know each other.

Lead in to writing: The pictures can serve as prompts to generate a brief autobiographical sketch.

▸ Biographical Drawings, Event Drawings

Social studies, literature, and more: Instead of drawing about themselves, students can illustrate the elements or characteristics of a historical period, a character in a novel, or a science experiment. Many things that can be communicated in words can be communicated—at least roughly or playfully—through pictures.

▸ Metaphorical Art

This is a drawing variation for middle school, higher-level thinking, and creative learners. The intent is to communicate your points metaphorically. Thus, with the autobiographical drawings discussed previously, suggest to your students that the elements in their drawings be symbolic or metaphorical. If you want to communicate that you like hot food, for example, you might draw a fire coming out of a dinner plate. To communicate that you like water, you might draw yourself as a fish. A sun in your picture must represent something other than a sun—perhaps a bright outlook or an appreciation for warmth.

▸ Abstract-Concept Art

Select a concept—e.g., life, happiness, the future, love. Students create an art form reflecting that concept. Have available a wide variety of materials and media from which students may choose.

Variations: (1) Encourage students to secretly choose any concept to express; when their art is finished, the other students try to guess the concept. (2) One student calls out a concept from a suitable list and the others depict it given a brief period of time, say 3 minutes. Then another student calls out a concept, and so on.

Possible concepts include the following: "Draw the clothing styles 100 years from now." "Create lines and shapes and colors as you listen to the music that is being played." Or with students in pairs, one student moves or dances to music while the other expresses that dance on drawing paper.

Map Drawing

This tool helps children learn and retain map features and geography in a playful format. First, display a map (e.g., state or country) on a table, a wall, or projected on a screen. Students work in pairs or small groups, carefully studying the map for a specified length of time (e.g., 2 to 3 minutes). The map is then removed or covered, while students cooperatively draw the map from memory. Repeat this process—displaying and then removing the map—at intervals to enable students to refine their maps. Within the student team, each student can specialize on particular features, e.g., natural, political, or general proportions. An alternative is to have one or more maps available at either end of the room; students may get up to study the maps whenever they choose, and then return to their seats to do the actual drawing from memory.

A key feature of this technique is that students will learn to rehearse the visual information over and over in their minds, to ensure that their short-term retention carries over just long enough to get that information down on paper. This repetitive short-term rehearsal then has a greater probability of making it into long-term memory. In addition, the actual process of drawing brings in another modality, and therefore, additional brain cells and neuron connections.

Spatial Conceptualization Drawings

Students draw the school as it would look from an airplane above. Or students predict and then draw a cross-sectional view of an apple or a kiwi prior to sectioning the fruit. Cut the fruit crosswise, and have the students check against their drawings.

Now, predict and draw the view if the fruit is cut differently—longitudinally or at an angle. These kinds of activities are brief, playful, and challenging, and they develop three-dimensional spatial thinking skills. Plus a child does *not* need to be good at language or math to succeed—yet another opportunity to nurture and validate the talents of as many children as possible.

Scale Drawings

Students draw something to scale, e.g., the room, their desk, a microscope. My students at a variety of grade levels enjoyed these tasks, and it was gratifying to see the level of attention many of them they put into the details.

Math: This is good experience with measuring, ratios/proportions, as well as visual/spatial practice.

Writing: Students draw a map of their bedroom or home, and then translate their map into a written description that conveys the desired image to a reader.

Desk Organization Blueprints

On a blank blueprint of their desk or locker, students will draw in the layout of the items stored in that space.

Now, here's the useful, challenging, and fun part . . .

Collect their "blueprints," and hand these back to the students at a later date. You then check that each student has a blueprint that matches the space. Each student has two options: (1) reorganize their desk to fit their blueprint, or alternatively, (2) create a new blueprint to fit the current state of their desk. Eventually—sooner for some children than others!—they learn to be more consistent and organized in putting things back in the same place.

Life skills, organization: Spatial organization tasks such as this one help students learn to be more organized with their materials and to know where they put things and when to throw things away. These tasks also give students practice developing a system and sticking to it.

■ Dramatization and Role-Playing

There are many concepts, skills, and problem-solving scenarios that can be dramatized in 5 or 10 minutes. A few interdisciplinary examples are below. Of course, do not forget opportunities to use costumes or puppetry, for example, when the urge strikes you.

Authentic Skills Dramatization

I had one of the parents role-play with me a telephone conversation where I needed to contact someone for information and write down what I learned. We purposely made it both informative and educational, and the kids very much enjoyed the performance. Of course, this led right into the research project we were doing in which these 7th graders would be using the phone.

Role-Plays for Rules, Procedures, and Problem-Solving

Use role-plays to model many of your expectations for routines. And use them for the problems that can and do happen throughout the school year: "He took my pencil." "They won't play with me." "This is boring."

Student responsibility: So often, children need to actually observe, or even role-play themselves, successful problem-solving. This is much less abstract than merely hearing the solutions verbally. Students truly enjoy role-playing the right and wrong ways to solve these problems: (1) the utterly antisocial and dysfunctional behaviors, and (2) the more responsible and polite alternatives.

Math Story Problem Dramatization

Math story problems are acted out. Teams of students invent and act out a math problem, which their classmates then convert simply into a solved arithmetic equation. For example, two children might simply dramatize one child starting with three pencils and then being handed another two. The classmates write on paper: "$3 + 2 = 5$".

Here's a higher-level dramatization. The scene is two children dramatizing being in a car, one of them driving.

> Autumn: "Alex, stop driving so fast."
> Alex: "But if I don't go 60 miles an hour, we'll never get there."
> Autumn: "Even if you only go 50 miles an hour, it shouldn't take us very long to go the 100 miles."
> Alex: "Well, how much sooner would we get there if we drove 60 the whole way?" (The solution might be depicted by writing the following: "At 50 mph, 100 miles/50 mph = 2 hours. At 60 mph, 100 miles/60 mph = 1.67 hours or 1 hour, 40 minutes. Thus, save 20 minutes at 60 mph.)

Process Dramatization

Students in groups act out a theme in nature, a technology, or a science process. You can have the performers do this without talking, and after the performance the class tries to guess what was performed. Dramatize the motions of the sun, earth, and moon to illustrate night and day, seasons, eclipses, etc.

Assessment: In the previous example, if the children can role-play the movements of the sun, earth, and moon, then clearly they've got the concept.

Even very complex, high school–level concepts can be dramatized. In biology, we've had students role-play biochemistry processes, such as protein synthesis.

Primary variation: You can have it be teacher-directed, where all students are simultaneously role-playing the same process. Possible choices include: act out a bird hatching from an egg; be a seed germinating and growing into a tree.

Characterization Role-Plays

Students role-play characters from history or from fictional stories they are reading. Place the chosen characters in a new setting; you can creatively combine characters from various sources. For example:

Charlotte (the spider from *Charlotte's Web*) is spinning a web in Abe Lincoln's log cabin, and the two characters are discussing . . .

Language arts and varied modalities: By incorporating the dramatization with the reading and learning, you add variety and enable students' minds to experience and process their learning using more parts of their brains.

Frozen Role-Play

Reading, literature, sharing: Students form groups of 3 to 5 members, and their director shares a story or true event. The group is then directed to re-create the climax of this story frozen in time (sort of like a 3-D snapshot); there is no action or talking in the production, just a frozen picture.

■ Music and Rhythm across the Curriculum

These are just a very few ideas to remind you of the potential.

Drum Roll

This is both delightful and quick, perfect for refocusing students during a transition time or to pick up the energy. You or one of your students is the conductor, and the other students are the drummers. As the conductor raises his or her arms, the students drum with palms on their desks or on their laps. The higher the conductor raises his or her arms, the louder the drumming. By raising and lowering the arms a number of times, there is a pleasant succession of louder and softer waves. Finally, quickly cross your arms to instantly halt the drumming—all eyes will be on you and the room will be completely silent!

Variation: Your right arm can signal the drumming for half the class and your left arm for the other half. Now you can move the two arms independently.

Music and Mnemonics

Students can sing the alphabet, spelling words, multiplication facts, etc. Music (as well as the rhythm of clapping or snapping fingers) can accompany the students' recital of number facts, parts of speech, European countries, etc. Rewrite verses of songs to reinforce what you are learning. Remember, if you have any musically talented students who create a wonderful new song that teaches something, you can use that song every year following.

Background Music

Different types of music can be used to predispose students to a particular mood or thinking style. Some classical music, for example, has been used to reduce math anxiety among students. Other types of music stimulate such areas as feelings, creativity, or high energy levels. The music itself can serve as the focus for the lesson—students can be asked to describe, compare and contrast, predict, discuss feelings about the music, etc.

Music as Learning Prompt

Language arts, writing: A piece of music can prompt students into writing their reaction to the music.

Social studies: Listen to a piece of music as a lead-in to a time period, geographic area, or culture.

Music to Build Relationships

Invite students to play instruments they have been practicing. Talk about music. Ask their opinions. Share favorites. Sing. Build some simple instruments, such as drums. Or use found objects to create your own spontaneous percussion orchestra for a Friday afternoon performance—this last idea would, of course, need to be videotaped.

■ Sensory Experiences

Bring in the tactile to foster greater engagement with a variety of your required learning outcomes. Enjoy reinforcing academic content with the feel of clay between your fingers, the balancing of mobiles, or the creativity of collages.

Everything is connected—the very act of a student following the recipe to make the modeling dough involves reading and measuring.

Tactile Writing

Students can write with their fingers: in shaving cream, or in a box with sand or rice; on each other's backs; in the air with their eyes closed; in a jar of water;

in foods such as puddings, yogurt, or ketchup. The textures—and in the last example, tastes—reinforce learning through greater sensory input.

Back-spelling partners: One child spells a word on their partner's back, who then says the letters out loud as the letters are felt.

Back-picture partners: Same as above, but instead of a word, a simple picture is drawn on the back. The perceived picture is drawn on paper as it is being felt.

Cut and Paste

This is something we have all done before—you cut out the separate parts of a picture, pattern, or project, and you paste them together in their correct positions. This simple activity will stimulate the visual-spatial-tactile/kinesthetic learning modes, thus providing another avenue for reinforcing the lesson content. It's relaxing and thoroughly enjoyable for many students, who find the opportunity to cut and paste to be a nice break from pencil and paper tasks. They especially enjoy being able to talk while doing this, so it's a pleasant opportunity for them to socialize while learning.

Sequencing skills, reading comprehension: For elementary students who are having difficulty with sequencing tasks, the children first read a photocopied paragraph or story, then they cut out each sentence (or paragraph), mix them up, and then place the pieces of paper back in their correct sequence.

Novel Manipulatives

You can include both visual and tactile elements into a predominantly left-mode task such as grammar. As one example, have children glue colored grains of rice to the appropriate words on a worksheet—e.g. yellow grains under nouns, blue grains under adjectives. Create a competition—the nouns against the adjectives—which will there be more of?

Sensory Novelty

There are so many experiences that nurture curiosity and engagement, especially for the younger children. I brought in cinnamon sticks, which are nothing more than bark off a cinnamon tree—kids were amazed and perplexed that cinnamon is bark. On another day, we munched on seaweeds. Or, I covered up the labels of items such as vanilla extract, and they had to sniff and guess. We mixed up cornstarch and water to make that solid/liquid goop that defies description. In the Pacific Northwest, where I live, we smelled wild critters that smell like almond extract (a millipede); a snail that smells like garlic; a berry that smells like bleach. I imitated birdcalls—my talent is doing crows. For a novel visual perspective, show children a highly magnified view of a dust mite—though this can be frightening to anyone under the age of ten!

Find things to touch, to smell, to listen to. There is such incredible novelty at the supermarket, in nature, and elsewhere.

Chapter 13
Learning for Life

A leader is best
When people barely know he exists,
Not so good when people obey and acclaim him,
Worst when they despise him.
But of a good leader, who talks little,
When his work is done, his aim fulfilled,
They will all say, "We did this ourselves."

Lao-tse

In this chapter you'll find a variety of tools for building students' *self-efficacy*. Self-efficacy is the confidence, knowledge, and actions to successfully achieve positive results. Self-efficacy is different from self-esteem. Self-esteem is feeling good about oneself. It is a positive *belief*. Self-efficacy is more; it is the *ability* to translate that belief into successful action.

One can have a healthy self-esteem, yet still not accomplish much. This is the especially troublesome outcome when teachers habitually praise children for very minor or trivial accomplishments. You do not want a child deceived into having confidence without skills or knowledge. What eventually happens is that next year, or after high school, this individual is forced to survive in a world where that praise is suddenly lacking, and the student has no skills or knowledge with which to succeed. I have seen this happen to children, and the results are not pleasant. These children become hurt, passive, and defeated, or else they become rebellious and blame others.

What's the solution? Encourage effort. Effort will always be an asset to one's success. Encourage perseverance. Encourage getting along with others, self-reflection, and positive expectations for oneself. And try to foster these things so that children free themselves from being dependent on outside praise for their self-worth.

Example: A child ties her shoe for the first time. Instead of saying "Good job," ask "How does that make you feel?" Or, a consistently disorganized fifth grader starts getting more organized. Say "I noticed your notebook today."

The development of students' self-esteem is certainly important. But the development of students' self-efficacy is perhaps our most important goal of all. You can foster students' self-efficacy by applying a number of the tools in this chapter.

■ AUTHENTIC LEADERSHIP ROLES

There are many opportunities throughout the year for students to take on more leadership and responsibility. These are situations where one or more students are fully capable of generating lesson ideas, initiating a discussion topic, designing a worksheet or math problem, and teaching a skill or activity.

Classroom jobs: Each child benefits from being given simple caretaking responsibilities. I was impressed with how much a child might enjoy heating up tea for others or vacuuming the floor or helping organize the pencils. Your students can help write a monthly newsletter to parents or write a welcome letter for next year's students and parents.

In one school in a small town, the kindergarten children decided they needed a crosswalk; they wrote a letter to the town hall and walked down to deliver it. They got their crosswalk. Another teacher's students wrote a persuasive letter to the principal to help solve a litter problem by having more trashcans.

Student products: Students can make things that have a real purpose, such as greeting cards and personalized stationery. When you encourage student initiative, you reduce your workload while increasing student learning. Here are some benefits.

Feedback that leads to better teaching: When students feel comfortable contributing their ideas and suggestions, they will work actively with you to make lessons more efficient and more enjoyable. This is much superior to a situation where your students just accept their fate and work passively with a lesson that may not be at all ideal.

Student responsibility and ownership: Students can be partners with you in actively thinking about ways to make things run even more smoothly in your classroom. For example, students can enjoy problem-solving how to clean up a spill, and take great pride in their own efforts. It becomes "our" classroom, rather than just the teacher's classroom.

Periodically, you may want to have students write up worksheets, quizzes, or assignments. When students create the assignments, they take more ownership of the task. The result is enhanced motivation and learning, as well as student empowerment.

Student and teacher enjoyment: You might occasionally ask students for their suggestions: "I haven't done this science experiment before. So definitely tell me which parts are better or not so good. If we want, we can just spend more of our time on the best parts."

■ STUDENT DECISION-MAKING AND GOAL-SETTING

The enormous range of choices available to us necessitates an equally great need to make decisions. The situation is made even more demanding by today's unprecedented rate of change—culturally, economically, politically, technologically. *Furthermore, when kids can make better decisions, we don't have to make those decisions for them! This cuts our workload.*

What you can and cannot change: Children need to know that it doesn't help to blame your predicament on the past, on your parents, or on your environment. Some things you can't change, like the weather or the past. Some things you can change, like your attitude or your behaviors.

Ingredients for Decision-Making

Decision-making can be more of an intuitive, gut-level act. And it can be a more sequential, logical-analytical one working with the parts. Intuitive decision-making is not easily teachable, because most of the process occurs out of reach of our conscious awareness. In contrast, the logical-analytical parts can be modeled and taught quite effectively. Here are six steps.

State a specific problem or question: Try to be clear. In other words, ask "What food should we feed the goldfish?" rather than "What should we do for the goldfish?" (This is very good training for children to learn to be more precise.)

Gathering information: Collect exactly the information or data that addresses your problem—no more, no less. Many students collect information just because it's there!

Set criteria and priorities: List the criteria to consider in making the decision. Decide which of those criteria is most important. Decide what needs to be done, and in what order. Decide these things based upon your goals and the time available.

List and evaluate alternatives: List the advantages and disadvantages of your alternatives. Things to think about: You may want to weight these according to the importance you give each criterion.

Make a decision: In making your decision, be willing to give up all other decisions. (Some kids will make a decision, and then continue for eternity reconsidering the decisions they had just rejected.) Thus, commit to the decision you made—this is harder than it sounds. Keep in mind that not making a decision is also a decision!

Take action: Follow through. Implement the decision. (Many kids will make a decision, but be too passive or frozen in fear to implement it.)

Infusing Students' Decision-Making across the Curriculum

When the appropriate context arises, you can integrate decision-making and goal setting into existing lessons and situations. This can be done often in 5 or 10 minutes. For example:

Vocabulary and process skills: Use the vocabulary of leadership and decision-making. Even with young children, you can say, "I like how you took the initiative to solve that problem." "You demonstrated self-reliance by not needing me to make that decision for you." "You really looked at alternatives." "Thank you for prioritizing." The best way to teach vocabulary is within the context of the present, teachable moment.

Social studies, literature: Look at the decisions and goals of historical figures, politicians, or fictional characters in a story. Ask the children whether they agree or disagree and why. Ask what goals they would have had in that situation.

Ask them to list the pros and cons, or to compare/contrast that person's actions with what theirs would be.

Writing: Share anecdotes from your own life of decisions and goals, and have students write about their own.

Math: Incorporate decision-making into authentic purchase decisions, e.g., the pros and cons of this toy versus that one, and the difference in cost.

Have students involved in decisions that affect them: These include classroom pets . . . field trips . . . guest speakers . . . project choices . . . assignment due dates . . . room arrangement . . . student jobs . . . design of centers.

Set expectations: Expect thoughtful, intelligent decisions from your students, and you're more likely to get them.

Provide opportunities for students to set their own goals: These might be goals that are slightly out of reach but not out of sight. This can be done daily, weekly, monthly, or for the entire year. Periodically, have students assess their progress toward these goals.

Encourage students to consider alternatives, and to prioritize those alternatives according to their own values and goals. For example, "Make a list of the next three topics or types of literature you want to read about, and put them in order with your favorite at the top. Then when we go to the library to select our reading, you will be more efficient."

Integrate within project-based learning: Teach your students the previously listed ingredients of decision-making prior to assigning projects or other independent work. Then have them apply decision-making to their actual schoolwork.

Plan B

This is a simple yet powerful tool for yourself and for your students. Whatever the task or problem, you've got an alternate "Plan B" should the first choice not succeed.

Classroom problems: Imagine a student who tends to socialize and not get work done. You meet one-to-one; the student suggests a solution, and you have your doubts that the student's suggestion will work. Nonetheless, *you can honor the student's idea, and at the same time pursue other solutions*, merely by asking for, or suggesting, a backup Plan B. (Simple, elegant, nonconfrontational, and fosters dialogue and trust.)

Have students generate Plan Bs with respect to planning their future; designing a project where there might be insufficient materials, money, or time; creating strategies for a basketball game; or planning a field trip. Always have a Plan B!

■ Assignment Menus

Create a menu of assignments and learning tasks from which students may choose. This menu might be for a particular time during the day or week (e.g., centers), or it might be for a longer-term project for middle school. Menus provide opportunities for students to experience choice, with the resulting responsibility, pride, and competence that can result from doing so wisely. Menu assignments are one method for validating . . . multiple intelligence talents . . . diverse student interests . . . different ability levels.

■ Project Packets

Instead of giving students one task at a time, why not present several tasks that students must manage more independently and self-reliantly. For students to succeed with these multiple tasks does require fairly substantial time management skills. Go slow—very gradually provide more responsibilities to the children to manage their time and their learning. Teach and reinforce these time management skills that are crucial in life. Examples: "Predict how long each of these three tasks will take you." "Look at the clock now. In 10 minutes, all of you should be working on the second assignment. Let's see how well you can do at checking the time, so that you do not have to depend upon me reminding you."

Assessment: The assessment rubrics can be incorporated readily within the packets, so children know exactly what is expected.

Time Management Logs

I have found these to be very effective with my 7th graders when they are engaged with a project packet, or other less structured "choice times." The time management log is just a single sheet of grided paper for each student, with these columns from left to right:

(1) Task I am working on (2) Time started (3) Time finished (4) Total time (#3 minus #2)

The beauty of these logs is that both the students and the teacher have a more accurate record of where all that time went. Example dialogue:

Teacher:	"It looks like you spent 45 minutes on just the first part. That seems like a lot of time."
Student:	"The time went by so fast."
Teacher:	"Do you think if you sat over there, you might get distracted less?"
Student:	"Yeah, that's a good idea."

■ Authentic Problem-Solving

Authentic modeling: Definitely model your own daily problem-solving, e.g., looking up a word in the dictionary when you are not sure of a meaning or spelling. At these times, it is superb strategy to think aloud as you problem-solve.

When you do make an error, admit it, and be willing to laugh at yourself. Or confidently explain how you made the mistake, and what you'll do to correct the situation. You'll make your job much easier as soon as you give up a need to be right!

Be alert to your non-verbal communication: Remember that students learn more from how we act than what we say.

Facilitate student thinking: Ask students "What will you do differently next time?" Or, "I wonder what we can learn from that?"

Share other successful role models: Orally, or through readings, explore the mistakes and problems that were successfully confronted by leaders and heroes of the past and present. It is especially fruitful to accumulate in your repertoire a knowledge of the students' own heroes, and to use these as examples.

Language arts: Students can interview a parent or other adult regarding important problems that person confronted, and decisions they made.

Current Issues Problem-Solving

Especially as children get older, they can certainly see that *adults are far from infallible in problem-solving*. Have your students share problem-solving and decision-making strategies as they apply to real-world problems. Ask "If you were the mayor of New Orleans, or the president of the United States, how would you have done things before and after the flooding?"

■ AUTHENTIC INVESTIGATIONS

This is an engaging, open-ended, student-centered task that integrates a variety of curriculum areas and learning objectives. Students pick from a list of products or services—anything from digital cameras to dog foods, frozen orange juice to open-heart surgery. Then brainstorm a list of meaningful questions concerning the selected item:

- What are the important features? What does it cost?
- Are there advantages to buying at one store versus another?
- Are there alternative products that might be effective substitutes?

The product or service is then researched using any appropriate source of information—parents, friends, store employees, books, Web sites. Students compile and summarize their results (either as a written, graphic, or oral presentation), and field questions from the other students.

As a highly practical, real-life skill, these investigations can be adapted by the teacher for any grade level and most subject areas. For example:

Primary: Facilitate these inquiries through discussion, by asking the children questions, and by thinking aloud as you model the thinking skills. For example, if you have a goldfish in an aquarium, the questions might include: "What should we feed the goldfish? How much should we feed it? How do we find out these answers?" You can even phone the pet store right then and there, and let the children listen in—or even have a child volunteer to help find the phone number in the Yellow Pages or ask one of the questions or have all the kids in unison say, "Thank you, Mr./Ms. Store Person."

Math: Students compare prices, calculate percent discounts, and compare savings by buying in quantity.

Language: The teacher emphasizes the quality of research and clear presentation of information.

Science: Choose topics related to curriculum. Environmental topics might include pesticides or recycling. Life science topics include goldfish, hamsters, or birdhouses. Health topics might include aspirin or flu vaccines. Obviously, the list could go on!

Social studies: Emphasize products or services that develop students' abilities to obtain information from the community, from business, or from government agencies.

Authentic Creativity with Products and Technologies

Creativity is a prominent part of the real world, not just a frivolous mental exercise for the end of the period. To illustrate, here are a selection of possibilities especially suited to middle school level—though you can adapt them for other grade levels easily.

These tasks will motivate authentic interdisciplinary learning, critical thinking, and consumer awareness—using all those junk mail catalogs of products that flood your mailbox.

First collect a small pile of catalogs for raw material. Each student or small group chooses (or is assigned) one product advertisement—a miniature TV, a graphite fishing rod, or a new computer game, for example. Ads for more novel or innovative products, especially ones with which we are unfamiliar, provide outstanding raw material for this exercise. Consider assigning students to find their own product to study.

Students examine the ad. At this point, depending upon your objectives and curriculum area, assign students to work on one or more versions of the following tasks.

Your Menu

Brainstorm: List ways that the technology might break, wear out, or function improperly. List ways the technology could be improved. List questions you would want to ask prior to purchase or use. Direct your questions to the inventor, the manufacturer, or the retail store. Brainstorm consequences of using the technology, including both the intended ones and unintended ones (i.e., side-effects). You may focus on the consequences for an individual consumer, or on the economic, political, or environmental consequences.

Evaluate or judge: Rate the product or invention. First develop criteria for your rating system. Why did you choose those criteria? How did the invention rate, and might different people come up with different ratings?

Draw creatively: Create a diagram of your own version of the product, the way you'd like to see it designed. Or sketch the inside of the invention, the way you might imagine it, whether realistically or creatively.

Create your own ad: Design an ad for this product for TV, radio, or print media. Include appropriate visuals, music and sound effects, colors, etc., to make your ad attractive, attention getting, and motivating to prospective customers.

Design a marketing plan: Who might purchase or need this product? Are there competing products already available, and if so, how could you persuade consumers to buy this one instead? What incentives could you provide to motivate a consumer to buy? How would you advertise, promote, and market the product?

Predict the product's future: Explore three alternative scenarios: best case, worst case, and your predicted outcome. Imagine a world where this product is commonplace. In what ways will the world be different as a result of this product? Be realistic or highly imaginative.

Write a story: Develop a plot based on this product. What if this product got into the wrong hands? Modify the product to make it more exciting in your story. Write up an imaginary interview between yourself and the product's inventor. Or imagine you are the product's inventor. Write an entry in your diary for the day that you first got the idea for this product.

Role-play: Perform a dramatization of one of the following: role-play the salesman for the company trying to sell the product to a gullible customer and to an aware customer; perform a skit (training video) that teaches new customers how to safely use the product.

Analyze or calculate: Determine the costs and benefits of this product for the consumer. Create your own math problems. For example, "If each TV is sold for an average profit of $108 each, and if three TV sets out of 50 are returned as defective before being fixed and resold (costing the company an extra $38 per returned set), what is the total profit made by the company for each 100 sets sold?"

Advertisements

Advertisements are an obvious and ever-present part of our world, and they offer numerous options for learning across the curriculum.

Language arts: Use informational advertisements to help students see how main points are communicated succinctly and persuasively. Design your own travel brochure, or radio or TV commercial. Or brainstorm and design ads for real or imagined products or services.

There are so many learning outcomes you might incorporate: writing persuasively, summarizing main ideas, using grammatical conventions, engaging the reader.

Art: Look for elements of art in advertisements, and evaluate them for esthetics and design.

Social studies, critical thinking: Students assess advertisements for elements of propaganda.

Authentic Visitors, Guest Experts, and Audiences

Bring into your classroom writers, lawyers, and scientists from the community; artists, local heroes, older individuals with long-ago personal histories to share; world travelers; someone with an interesting pet. In addition to having these visitors present material and share with the children, they can also be an audience for the children.

■ INFORMATION LITERACY

Consider how much information is available on the Internet—and how much of it is redundant, trivial, biased, or inaccurate. *Successful individuals of the future will increasingly depend upon their information literacy—the ability to locate, process, and use information effectively.* The overwhelming bulk of information being produced in this global age must be carefully screened, skimmed, and often discarded.

Authentic news requests: Ask students questions such as these (where you really do want the answer): "Did anyone hear the weather forecast for tomorrow?" "Does anyone know who won yesterday's basketball game?"

Four Simple Tools to Facilitate Information Literacy

Here are just a few tool examples to get you started, or to refresh your memory.

Error searches (page 97): Within a playful context, purposely plant extraneous and inaccurate information or details within a variety of learning tasks (math story problems, sample essays or stories, giving directions). Your students will enjoy finding your "mistakes."

Collaborative note-taking (page 124): This is a wonderful note-taking technique that helps children listen for, and record, the pertinent ideas in their own words.

Search tasks: (pages 12, 96): You or your students create a list of information to locate online. The goal is to find accurate information quickly. For example: "Should a person take vitamins?" "What is the cheapest airfare next month from here to London?" "How far is it from my house to downtown?" "What is the bus schedule?"

Thinking aloud (page 43): With all students, and especially with younger children, think aloud with them when solving real problems that require information. "I need to buy a birthday present for my 5-year-old daughter. I wonder how late the store stays open tonight. Maybe the store's phone number is in the telephone directory."

■ NOTE-TAKING FOR ANY AGE

"Take notes." We've heard that line many times. But, what *is* the purpose for taking notes? In life—the real world—that purpose is to enable recall of information or ideas at a later time. It's very simple. The main purpose for taking notes in life is *not* to make them pretty for someone else (i.e., the teacher) or to write down what another person (the teacher!) thinks is important.

To help students develop lifelong note-taking skills, the following suggestions may help.

Get students to take notes in real life situations—such as getting price information on fishing gear or getting movie or bus schedules over the phone or taking notes on directions for an assignment.

Teach students to manage their notes—such as putting dates on pages, organizing notes according to date or subject, and deciding on a consistent location for keeping them.

Encourage both note-taking skills and management of notes by cueing students as to when notes may be useful, *not* repeating directions over and over again; giving open notes tests and quizzes; and assigning projects that require practice of note-taking skills.

Playful Picture Note-Taking

The kids love this one! I will ask kids to incrementally add elements to a picture as I describe a simple scene. "Picture a house. There is a bird on the roof. It is a sunny day, and there is one cloud in the sky. There are two windows on the front of the house."

Children of any age are amazed at how well their brains retain the information in their picture. Some students excitedly remind me 2 weeks later that they remember the scene. I use this activity to reinforce the importance of creating pictures to help us understand things better, or to solve math problems, for example.

For contrast, I will often ask students to memorize a series of random digits—7, 4, 2, 9, 3, 8. What thoroughly impresses the students is the contrast between their easy retention of a picture, compared with the complete lack of retention of the random digits. Our memories are helped when the information is visual and meaningful.

Social studies, science, etc: Have children draw picture notes to help them remember the content.

Math: Enjoy laughing with the kids as they all share their illustrations of a math story problem. Post these on a wall. Or in reverse: Children create and illustrate a story problem, and other students try to guess (or invent) the math story that would go with the illustration.

Key-Word Note-Taking

Key-word note-taking is the most effective method for stimulating retention of information at a later date. When we write only the few key words, rather than long phrases and sentences, our notes facilitate more learning and recall.

Collaborative Note-Taking Technique

This simple and powerful tool enhances motivation and retention by engaging students in more active processing of information. Here are the steps:

1. *Get their attention:* Think of a topic that you want to teach, or need to teach. Students, in small groups, are asked to generate possible answers to any interesting question on this topic. This stage uses the power of the hypothesize/estimate/predict tool described earlier.
2. *Present Information:* Orally, or in writing, present the information that addresses the question. Several minutes is good.
3. *Note-taking:* While the information (step 2) is being presented, students take notes. In order to hold all students accountable, each should be required to take notes, not just one student per group.
4. *Editing:* After the information has been presented, students are given several minutes to go over their notes with their group members and fill in details they may have missed, as well as correct for errors.
5. *Whole class sharing:* When groups are finished, two or three individual students share their notes with the entire class. As this stage proceeds, all students should be revising or editing their notes for clarity.
6. *Assessment:* I have found that open-note tests work superbly here. Students' note-taking efforts are positively reinforced for the appropriate reason—to facilitate recall of information at a later time. You will probably want to give the open-note test one or more days after the note-taking, perhaps even a few weeks later.

Micro-Notes

We would do well to avoid the commonly used pejorative term "cheat sheets" for this activity. As a means of studying for a test, students are allowed to use notes written on a single 1-inch square sheet (or larger if you prefer), to be stapled to the test when the test is collected. Micro-notes are excellent for constraining students to really think about the key words or main ideas. And because the student will have to decide what is important, thinking happens.

Effort and success: Students who will normally not study at all for a test will often do so if micro-notes are allowed.

Higher-level learning: This technique also enables you to avoid testing purely at the knowledge level, but instead to incorporate learning objectives at higher thinking levels.

Answer-to-Question Review

Provide an answer related to the content you are reviewing. Students then generate an appropriate question. You can have students work in pairs, with partners alternately switching roles, with first one and then the other creating answers. Or do this as a whole class; you give an answer and all students generate the questions.

■ Dialogue to Foster Self-awareness and Self-reliance

Child-centered dialogue has been discussed previously. It is so critical that I bring it up again. Talk with your students often. Whether you do it as a whole class as part of the school day, or one-to-one in the hall or at lunch, explore with them their perceptions and assumptions about their abilities, about school, about various issues. Do not just assume, for example, that your students know the seriousness of bullying, and how hurtful it can be. Do not just assume that each child knows that there is a relationship between one's effort and one's success. Students accumulate a vast array of misconceptions and unusual (to us!) perspectives. It certainly helps to find out what's going on in those brain cells of theirs.

Self-discipline and Responsibility Questions and Role-Plays

Expand your repertoire of questions that stimulate students' awareness of responsibility, leadership, and teamwork.

When a child is behaving inappropriately, ask "How does that help you?" "What are you going to do?" "Tell me your plan. Do you want some ideas?" "What will you do to improve things?" "How did you feel about your group? Did you want to be your group's leader? Were you able to contribute your own ideas, or did you feel pressured to just go along with what others suggested?" "Do you feel OK about asking questions when you get stuck?"

Role-play responsible behaviors and attitudes. Ask children, whole group or one-to-one, to model with you such concepts as respect, being patient, and disagreeing politely. It can be beneficial to do a role-play for both the presence and the absence of the desired behavior. Role-play scenarios such as (1) someone takes your seat, (2) your science project gets knocked onto the floor, or (3) someone keeps telling you the answers, and you would rather they didn't.

Character discussions: Pick a character, either fictional or nonfictional. Ask "Would this person make a good father? Or a good principal for our school? Or a fun person to be around?" Ask for students to elaborate on their answers, e.g., "Why do you say that?"

Thinking aloud: When you catch yourself being less responsible yourself, verbalize it with the kids: "Oh, I'm sorry; I didn't let you finish what your were saying." "I really need to work extra hard today to be patient and polite, because I didn't get enough sleep last night."

Personal Attributes and Vocabulary

Teach useful vocabulary to enlarge students' awareness of their attitudes, behaviors, and emotions. Words and concepts such as self-reliance . . . procrastination . . . compromise . . . accepting responsibility . . . being proactive . . . respect . . . nervous . . . reflective . . . jealous . . . hurt . . . pride . . . confidence. You might decide in advance those you will teach, or just introduce them as they happen within the context of the classroom.

Middle school language arts: Have students list (1) emotion words and (2) personality traits. Apply these words throughout the year with one-on-one dialogue with students, writing assignments, or describing characters within their readings.

You can list words and attributes of responsible learners and post the list on the wall. Verbally notice and acknowledge when students demonstrate those attributes. Likewise, students can brainstorm their expectations of responsible teachers or other adults.

Student-Initiated Service

Each student decides on a task that he or she can do for a family member, friend, or community organization. The student then writes this task (e.g., doing the dishes after dinner each day this week) on a blank coupon. The child gives the coupon to the appropriate individual, and this receiver of the coupon is then entitled to the free gift (i.e., task) specified on the coupon. (Adapted from Borba, 1988)

■ RELAXATION AND STRESS REDUCTION

The world's a stressful place to be, so it makes sense that all of us—teachers and students—have strategies to cope better with it. Here are some activities and strategies to consider. Here are a few techniques to try.

There are many stress-reduction techniques to choose from, both for yourself and your students. You might opt for building a small repertoire on your own, or you can choose a more integrated and structured routine based upon yoga, mediation, martial arts, or sports. You may also want to refer to the repertoire included within "Brain Gym" (Dennison and Dennison, 1989).

Breathing

There are numerous variations of breathing exercises, most of which encourage slow, deep breathing. One technique to try is counting breaths—close your eyes, then count to yourself each time you inhale starting at one. When you get to ten, start over at one, and repeat the process.

Yawning

When you yawn, as when you breathe deeply, you can relieve stress. Try yawning intentionally—frequently, a forced one or two will grow spontaneously into a full-blown series of wonderful tension-releasing yawns. This is especially contagious and entertaining in groups.

Tense and Relax

Slowly tighten up your muscles, hold the tension for several seconds, and then release. Repeat two or three times. Try this technique especially with areas that tend to hold tension, such as your hands, face, neck, shoulders, and back. You need less than a minute or two of free time to do this with students.

This can also be fruitful when interacting one-to-one with a child who is having a difficult moment; in this case, it is best if the child already has practiced the technique during a calmer time.

Say, "relax" to yourself: This helps your nervous system create a subconscious association. By saying the word "relax," one can actually cause one's nervous system to do so.

Stretching and Movement

As with tense and relax, this takes only a few moments. Examples include rolling your head back and forth, or side to side; rotating, lifting, and dropping your shoulders; and various types of stretches of the arms, legs, and torso.

Aerobic Exercise

Activities that raise pulse and breathing rate—running, swimming, bicycling, and many sports—are beneficial in numerous ways. They improve physical health and resistance to disease, decrease tension, and enhance one's feeling of well-being via the body's production of endorphins. Unfortunately, many children are already far too sedentary.

Sometimes, one or more students will really need to work off some extra energy—have them jump rope, or even just jump up and down, for several minutes at an appropriate time.

Authentically Teaching and Modeling It

Authentically model stress-reduction techniques: For example, after an especially stressful commute through traffic, tell the kids you need a moment to take a few deep breaths. Or say, "Boys and girls, I'm going to put this relaxing music on now, because it's been a stressful day."

Share your own stories that illustrate how you have relieved tension in your own life.

Demonstrate one or more stress reduction or relaxation techniques with students, especially in an informal setting in the hallway or at recess.

Ask students to teach you a relaxation method or stretch. Especially with middle school kids, there will be one or more who have their favorite (or difficult!) stretch or movement to share.

Section 3
Your Repertoire, Your Wisdom, and Your Orchestration

Teaching is, of course, far more than knowing lots of stuff you can do with kids. It is about the orchestration, which is where your wisdom enters. The chapters in this section aim to tap your wisdom and to extend it in directions you may not have anticipated. Each chapter approaches different facets of this challenge—with commonsense strategies and insights that give you the maximum payoff from your repertoire, and from your scarcity of time. These chapters are all about taking your repertoire to the next level.

Chapter 14
Your Repertoire in Action

This is the chapter you absolutely do want to read carefully.

It is all too easy to settle for a smaller repertoire, even though a larger one will give you more enjoyment and success. This chapter presents two very simple ideas for expanding your repertoire to make teaching easier, more enjoyable, and more successful—and to accomplish these things with minimal effort.

■ TRIAL RUNS

Whenever you are thinking of trying out a new teaching strategy or activity, it is best to experiment small-scale. You want to try something new where it will do the least amount of damage if it fails. These first attempts, or trial runs, can be attempted in one or more of the following ways:

- Last few minutes before lunch or the end of the day
- Outside of class with your favorite students
- As a separate mini-lesson, and not as an essential part of a larger unit
- At a time when you and your students are getting along especially well

Why Are Trial Runs So Important?

When you try something new that doesn't succeed, your brain can too readily attach itself to those negative memories. The emotional part of your brain then inhibits you from trying new ideas in the future. Your positive belief in both yourself and your students suffers extra wear and tear.

Furthermore, because teaching already involves stress, you do not want to add any more of it. It is supremely better if you design your teaching so that (1) you freely try new ideas and grow professionally and personally as a result, and (2) you minimize the emotional cost of this growth. Basically, you want to grow while minimizing the discomfort that this growth sometimes entails.

Trial runs—a (very!) simple idea that works.

■ THE POWER OF A REMINDER LIST

Imagine you had 60 seconds to recall any and all movies you've seen in the past five years. Where would you start? Where in your brain would you find movie titles? The answer is this: unlike a computer or a reference book, *there is no index to your brain*. You have no quick, reliable method for accessing what is in there. It's hit-or-miss, it's random, and it's inefficient. This means you will have perfectly useful knowledge related to teaching that your brain will not be able to find when you need it.

Most of you have poor recall. This is especially true if you are busy or under stress. The result is that your repertoire tends over time toward having fewer and fewer tools that you use more and more often. This is because any tool you use today predisposes you to access more habitually that same teaching tool tomorrow.

An Index to Your Brain

One of the easiest ways to improve your teaching is simply to create on a single sheet of paper an index of key reminder words to trigger your recall. Keep a copy of this index or reminder list in your lesson plan book, and another copy taped near your desk.

Anytime you are attending an education workshop, or skimming education materials or journals, add key word reminders for any strategies or activities that you want to apply in your classroom. The sole purpose of the reminder list is to make it likely that you will use more of what you already know.

How to Create Your Reminder List

Record only those key words that you will easily recognize at a glance. Do not put something on your reminder list unless you will quickly recognize it next week or next month.

Your reminder list will grow. Decide upon categories for your tools so that you can find what you are looking for in five or ten seconds. Here are some categories teachers have found useful: lesson starters, review and practice, quick fun, team-building, content areas (e.g., language arts, math), multiple intelligence, circle time activities, end of day. Some tools will fit more than one category.

"Succinct Wisdom" Reminder Sheet

In addition to tool reminders, keep another list of those eloquent bits of wisdom that you come across. Certain authors of education materials, or self-help books, for example, are supremely quotable. Jim Fay and David Funk's *Teaching with Love and Logic* (1998) could single-handedly give you a whole page of wisdom reminders: "A positive self-concept comes from feeling capable"; "The more we try to make someone change, the more likely we are to lock them into the offending behavior."

Use Sticky Notes

In addition to your reminder list, it is very helpful to place sticky note reminders within individual lesson plans. Your goal is to make it as likely as possible that you will actually incorporate the simple, and often quick, tools that can transform your teaching.

Just jot down each great new idea—especially a simple one—on a sticky note. And then pop it into your plan book. A guaranteed reminder.

Remember . . .

Each year you will accumulate more and more ideas and highlighted books, such as this one. Despite your best intentions, these will mostly collect dust on shelves with their buddies—hence their name of *dust buddies*. Dust buddies do not improve your teaching. You tend to get busy, and forget to refer back to those great ideas you once highlighted.

So, please . . . *use your reminder list!*

Chapter 15
Upward Spirals

Your physical and emotional wellness is a foundation for nearly everything else in your teaching (and your life). Remember, you're rather useless when you're . . .

> exhausted, impatient, irritable, overwhelmed, ill, angry, resentful, pessimistic, short-tempered, absent-minded, uncreative, slow-witted, overly serious, nervous, agitated, excitable, restless, unfocused, hurried, thin-skinned, touchy, testy, fidgety, over-sensitive, wasted, drained, fatigued, consumed, wearied, empty, tired, spent, jaded, rushed, depressed, cynical, debilitated, feeble, or listless.

Therefore, make it a priority to enjoy your job—at least most days—and to design your life so that you thrive year after year. Your job is a marathon, not a sprint.

And this leads to the concept of the spiral.

■ THE TWO DIRECTIONS TO THE SPIRAL

There are two directions your life can spiral, and virtually all of us have experienced both of these. Here's the upward spiral . . .

You have a teaching day that goes extremely well, which inspires your enthusiasm and optimism, which energizes your body language and tone of voice, which improves the rapport you have with your students, causing them to be more engaged and learn more, which reduces your stress and your workload, so that you are more efficient, productive, and energetic with housework and other obligations that evening. You sleep soundly and are therefore prepared and energized for the next teaching day, which continues the momentum for this upward spiral.

The downward spirals are treacherous. For example, discipline problems within the classroom cause you to be impatient and stressed, which adversely affects your enthusiasm and your teaching style, which makes you less effective as a teacher, which affects your self-worth, which is communicated to students whether you like it or not, which causes you to dwell on school problems, which causes your sleep quality to deteriorate. And so forth.

■ Laws of the Spiral

What you want to keep in mind are these two universal truths:

These spirals tend to perpetuate themselves. A downward spiral keeps spiraling downward, and an upward spiral tends to make your life better and better.

The spiral that happens in the classroom will infect—for better or worse—the spiral that happens for you with the rest of your life. And the reverse is also true.

■ What to Do Now

Balance and enjoyment: Put yourself first. No, this doesn't mean ignoring your students' needs. It means conserving your energy, being assertive about your own needs, enjoying teaching, laughing, and pursuing outside interests. It means making it a goal to more fully enjoy your work and your life—not one or the other.

There's more job than there is you: Time is your scarcest resource. You must strategically act to allocate your time. Focus on those efforts that give you the greatest return. The ideas in this book will make it easier for you to do this.

Acceptance: Know that you'll never get every kid to be a happy, well-adjusted, educated human being. Heck, it's hard enough getting ourselves to be happy, well-adjusted, educated human beings. By accepting this reality, you are taking the first step toward greater enjoyment and success.

■ Igniting and Sustaining Upward Spirals—Instantly

There are a number of simple actions you can take to immediately improve your day. Here are three.

Endorphin Replays

Endorphins are the "runner's high" chemicals that your body produces when you are entirely engaged in the present. Whenever you have a splendid moment in the classroom or in your life, be sure to share that moment later in the day or week with a colleague, student, or friend. In this way, you rekindle the same physiological high you experienced the first time. Flood your mind/body system with positive chemicals every chance you get. Example: Something funny happens with my 1st graders at 8:00 AM, and we all laugh. Just before lunchtime, I remind my kids of the funny incident, and—sure enough—we laugh again.

Three-Minute Actions

You won't be "up" every day. Do not wait for students to cheer you up—some days you might have to wait a long time. Take the initiative to interact with a favorite student, do something playful that will make you and students laugh, share a pleasurable incident that will give you an endorphin replay. Create the physiological state you want to be in, rather than just passively waiting for it to happen. And make yourself smile on those off days. When you smile you not only change the moods of others, but amazingly, you also improve your own mood. It isn't easy to be down and smile at the same time.

Personal Celebrations

This is a specific, concrete example of both an endorphin replay and the 3-minute action. Spend a short time with a student you enjoy, one who is learning and successful. By emotionally celebrating the students you *are* reaching, you improve your own sense of competence and your enjoyment. And you reduce your stress. Now you are better equipped to tackle your greater challenges.

Chapter 16
Three Mental Maps

The assumptions and perspectives you carry with you strongly influence your teaching. These "mental maps"—or paradigms, or philosophies—are not always readily apparent to us. Three examples will be explored here. You will no doubt see the enormous impact of your mental maps on your own teaching. The key is to be self-reflective and open to learning from your own life experiences and the ideas of others.

■ "Don't Take It Personally"

Your maps drive your thoughts and your behavior. As an example, consider Sandra, a 3rd grade teacher. She has a student who is frequently angry. Sandra's map tells her not to take it personally. Clearly, the anger is part of a larger issue in this child's life. So Sandra is patient and pleasant day after day after day. Sandra is still assertive, but she stays calm. Sandra knows that this child needs caring and a good listener, and not a daily dose of punitive consequences. The angry child does not get to her. Instead, Sandra works to build a relationship. Three months later, the child has made a complete turnaround in Sandra's class. Sandra's map is reaffirmed. Her next encounter with a troubled child will once again be met with thoughtfulness and caring.

■ "Believe in Yourself"

Jorge teaches 7th-grade social studies. Jorge's map tells him that a child who believes in himself will achieve so much more in school and in life. Jorge knows this because his own life taught him so. Jorge's map influences his teaching in numerous ways. His words and his body language communicate to his students the importance of perseverance. He constantly seeks opportunities to nurture positive self-talk in these children. It doesn't sound like a lecture to these kids, because it comes from Jorge's heart. And the children want to believe in him as well. He becomes their hero. Jorge's map is reinforced. Next school year, his inspiring message to his students will be as strong and passionate as ever. Maps have a way of doing this—whatever maps you carry in your mind tend to become ingrained over time. So choose your maps carefully.

■ "Patience, Persistence, and Optimism"

Marci doesn't spend her time predicting which 3rd graders can be taught and which can't, which kids will succeed and which won't. Instead, she just gives each day, and each child, her best effort. And she enjoys herself. She chooses not to worry about it. You do what you can do, you are not God, and you do not get the power to succeed with each child merely because you care and you know lots of good teaching strategies. Marci's map is one of good-natured, hard-working, persevering optimism. At the end of a year, and certainly 10 years later, Marci sees the incredibly positive influence she has had on a number of her students. But she didn't "save" all of them. Her map allows her to make her best effort, to accept her limitations, and to know that her own emotional wellness is the source of her tremendous gifts as a teacher.

Acceptance—that's the answer. You are not God. Give it your best effort while also investing in your own enjoyment of life. Some students will respond well. Some students respond less so, or appear to respond not at all. Of course, the impact you have made on another human life is not always visible, and it is not always immediate. Believe in yourself. Be patient with yourself. Know that you do *not* have control over the destiny of each child. That is the reality. Let your self-talk celebrate your successes, because these will inspire you and make you increasingly effective. *When your self-talk dwells on the students you are not reaching, you run the risk of making yourself miserable.* If that happens, your attitude, your energy, your teaching style, and your nonverbal body language will all sabotage your rapport with students as well as the quality of your lessons. Therefore, let the children you *are* reaching provide you with the emotional resilience, confidence, and joy to invest that needed energy in your more challenging students.

Again, accept that your job presents some extraordinary challenges. Suddenly it's a far more manageable job.

Chapter 17
Playing Around . . . Seriously

Insert novelty and variety into your routines.

Routines are essential to create a safe, efficient, productive, and pleasant learning environment. Novelty, variety, and play are also essential if learning and motivation are to be optimal. The advantages of a playful attitude are many, and this spirit of play can be integrated readily into any classroom.

Anything new or novel stimulates students' brains to engage as well as retain. So does humor. When routines are too fixed and too predictable, student learning diminishes. And you need this newness yourself to be more present and alive with the kids. This is especially true if you have been teaching for a number of years. Needless to say, when you're alive, you're more charismatic and effective than when you're in a detached autopilot state.

■ PACKAGE IT AS PLAY

Play is not an activity: it's a frame of mind, it's an attitude. Perhaps one could say that it's the epitome of intrinsic motivation.

Play comes in many forms. Some students are playing while skateboarding. Others play while writing essays or doing difficult math problems. One person's work is another's play.

Play is low risk: Through play, children eagerly participate in new situations, even challenging ones. They enjoy themselves without being self-conscious. They risk making mistakes. What is going on here that can be readily applied to the classroom? And, even better, can play be incorporated into your existing curricula and teaching style?

Play presents ideal opportunities for informal assessment: When children are absorbed in a playful task, their motivation is optimal and their stress level is minimal. Under these conditions, you can look at any child's efforts and see their actual cognitive and developmental capabilities. If, however, students are working at tasks that do not interest them, or that stress them too heavily, you are not really seeing their capabilities at all. You have the best opportunities for assessment when a child is in a state of maximum enjoyment. Because now you know that the student's performance at a task is not affected by lack of trying.

Create a climate conducive to play: This playful attitude is freer to emerge when the classroom is one of high trust and low risk. Incorporate play, and you nurture a high-trust, low-risk classroom climate. Likewise, create a high-trust, low-risk classroom, and the children will excel in their learning if you include play.

Introduce academic skills and content through play: Humor, novelty, and a spirit of playfulness are extraordinarily effective avenues for introducing new skills and concepts. Play can generate so many positive outcomes—student participation, responsible behavior, ownership of learning, thinking skills, and enhanced retention.

You have less paperwork: When students are truly absorbed in play, they are more likely to be involved in the learning task, so you do not have to threaten them with collecting and grading that particular assignment.

Humor and laughter are extremely powerful. Laughter can lower blood pressure for an hour or more; it activates endorphin levels and stimulates your thymus gland, which is connected to your immune system. Yes, a smile changes your brain and your body—it's very good medicine for you and your students.

Work hard, yes . . . but play hard, too. If you or your administration finds the word *play* too nonacademic, then call it by other labels. You can refer to it as *child-centered learning* or *intrinsic motivation*. It has been labeled by psychologists as a *flow state* and by coaches of Olympic athletes as a *peak performance state*.

Ten Opportunities to Teach with Novelty, Variety, and Play

1. Start of day for getting kids motivated
2. End of day to celebrate a sense of togetherness
3. Slow times for picking up energy
4. Happy times for enhanced sharing and positive strokes
5. Hyperactive times for releasing excess energy
6. Transitions for a change of pace or to lighten things up
7. Instructional times with new or difficult concepts or skills
8. Breaks from graded lessons as a sponge activity
9. Community-building times for positive attitudes
10. Opportunities to transfer from classroom lessons to "real world"

Chapter 18
Your Underachievers

Nearly every teacher has several or many students who are learning far below their potential. Some of these students consume our attention and our energy.

In this chapter, we will explore some simple, pleasant, and powerful strategies that can become key elements of your repertoire. As in previous chapters, the emphasis is on focusing your energy in ways that are enjoyable to both you and the students, and add minimally to your workload.

■ CHALLENGE AND CHOICE

Two of the decisions you make in your teaching that have enormous ramifications are (1) The amount of challenge—the degree of difficulty—of your lessons, and (2) the degree of choice students have within your classroom. How you orchestrate these two decisions affects *everything else*—your workload, student attitudes and learning, the direction of your "spiral," your inspiration, and the quality of your life.

It makes a great deal of sense to think very, very substantially about both challenge and choice in your classroom. A discussion of some key ideas follows. Following that are a collection of strategies you will find can have an extraordinary impact on your teaching. And these strategies are simple and satisfying.

Kids Do Want Challenge . . . Sometimes

You just need to know why and when. We hear lots of talk about many kids not wanting to work or think. This is only partly true. When kids are playing they do *not* take the easiest route, but instead seek challenge. They seek challenge because it provides greater enjoyment and satisfaction than easy tasks. As long as the context feels inviting rather than intimidating, kids will choose challenge over easy success.

Why then is the situation often not like that in school? Because in school, unlike play, it counts: they get graded, their self-esteem is on the line, and they rarely get to *choose* their challenges.

Kids Need Challenge . . . Sometimes

Challenge, when voluntarily sought, is exceedingly motivating and empowering. A challenging task can potentially produce the greatest gains in learner enjoyment, learning, and self-esteem. *Making an effort is one of the most important habits a child can learn in school,* for it is this habit that serves as a foundation for success and fulfillment through all of life.

Furthermore, the real world is not generally a forgiving place. Students must learn to persevere because not all solutions come easily.

Lastly, many challenging tasks are ideal contexts for cooperative learning, whereas many easy tasks might just as well be done individually.

High-Trust, Collaborative Environments Are Ideal

A student will opt for greater challenge when (1) the child has positive relationships within the classroom, (2) the choices are student-centered (i.e., appealing), and (3) the child has some level of confidence with the task.

Everything is connected. You can see that one of your core investments is to build relationships and trust. This is certainly one of the first and best ways to be more effective, to cut your workload, and to enjoy yourself—in other words, to achieve your upward spiral.

Decide Upon the Appropriate Choices

Allowing students to have some control over their learning is a primary factor in sustained achievement (Funk and Fay 1995, 150).

First, choice stimulates motivation and ownership of learning. And each of these will result in greater learning and retention. Therefore, whenever it will be a win-win situation, definitely allow students an appropriate selection of choices. The key word here is *appropriate*; you're in charge of the choices to be given. And you want those choices to be win-win so that you do not overwhelm yourself with additional paperwork or a chaos of management stresses.

Second, the real world is full of choices. Being able to handle choices effectively is one of the most important life skills students can acquire in school. Third, managing choice leads to self-awareness, self-esteem, and responsible behavior. And lastly, a range of choices enables students to approach their learning in ways that validate their talents and interest.

It may seem at first counterintuitive, yet choice can readily nurture perseverance. Because when the learner has control over the level of challenge, that learner is more willing to take on more difficult tasks. Giving students more control gives them more power. Children with power are more likely to persevere than children who feel helpless and dependent.

Keep in mind that many children are unaccustomed to choice—go slow.

■ SELF-INDIVIDUALIZATION VIA CHALLENGE WITH CHOICE

Within any classroom, whatever task you assign will usually be too challenging for some children and too easy for others. You run into the problem of having some students stressed, others bored or learning far below their ability, and a few fortunate souls experiencing the desired runner's high.

Whatever the task, it is crucial that you find ways to offer the learning at a variety of levels and to train your students to choose the level that best matches their ability and willingness for challenge. In other words, you train your students to *self-individualize*.

Your goal is for students to choose that level of challenge that not only maximizes their learning but also provides them with maximum enjoyment. This is not a naïve ideal—it can be achieved readily in a wide variety of ways. The examples to follow illustrate this "challenge with choice" strategy in action.

Challenge with Choice Strategy #1: Teacher-Friendly Choices

Provide students repeatedly with choices such that whichever alternatives are chosen, you are comfortable with the students' decisions. By nurturing students' decision-making opportunities often, you are building their self-efficacy. The more decisions children make, the more proficient they become—and the more eager they are—at making appropriate decisions. You are also building community and trust.

Let your wisdom dictate when to let students choose where to sit, how to decorate the room, and even when to have particular assignments due. These decision-making dialogues can be brief, random events, or you can design them into the regular weekly schedule.

Challenge with Choice Strategy #2: Posted Answers

With many lesson activities (e.g., worksheets) you can post the answers at one or more locations within the room. (Alternatively, each student or table group can have access to an answer sheet. Or have an "answer corner" in the room.) Encourage students to check the answers if and when they need to. You can maintain a rule that only one or two students are checking at a time, if you prefer. This is a simple technique with so many multiple, simultaneous benefits:

> *Knowledge of results:* Students receive more immediate feedback exactly when *they choose* to receive it, thus ensuring more ownership and better retention of the correct answer.
>
> *Level of difficulty:* Each student has control and ownership for the level of challenge he or she is willing to take on. This reduces stress for many learners—especially those who are at-risk—thus facilitating their participation and motivation. And it provides a higher level of challenge for capable and confident learners, who will choose to check their answers only at the very end to confirm their correctness (and be in charge of their own runner's high, rather than waiting for teacher praise).
>
> *Your time:* This strategy frees up more of your time to help slower learners, or to provide enrichment, or to enjoy some one-to-one time with a favorite student. Furthermore, it saves you the effort and time of grading papers, either outside of class or as a whole-class activity.
>
> *Pacing:* Posting answers enables students to work at their own pace. This is better than having the faster learners being bored while the slower learners are being frustrated.

> *Self-managing:* It nurtures students' autonomy as learners. They will gain more control of their own thinking, referred to as *metacognition*. Posted answers help children to become self-managing and more self-reliant.
>
> *Process:* Posting the answers frees you to focus your students more on the learning process, and not just on the answer. However, you should know that this process focus occurs *only if* you facilitate the lesson with this emphasis in mind.
>
> *Relationships:* By posting the answers you communicate that you are on the same team as your students—you're an ally, not an adversary. This is so important with some at-risk children.
>
> *Learning community:* All of the above help create a more relaxed learning environment with a sense of community.

Oh, and yes, some students—remarkably few—will just copy the answers and make minimal effort to actually learn the intended material. Do not give up the strategy just because of these few students. As the above list suggests, most students and the teacher are benefiting enormously. Just talk one-to-one to the few students who are ignoring or abusing the privilege. Use your wisdom pleasantly and patiently to troubleshoot with each of these students. Your own supportive, nonverbal communication, including your body language and tone of voice, will usually win them over.

Challenge with Choice Strategy #3: Invitational Choices

You can package more challenging tasks in ways that minimize the risk for students. Here are some examples:

While practicing math problems, ask the class "Do you want a difficult one?" Many students will say yes. Remind the others that because it is a difficult problem, they may choose to just watch.

"Do 10 of the math problems on page 28. The ones at the bottom of the page are much more challenging—please try at least one of those."

"When you finish the science experiment, try changing one of the variables and see what happens differently."

"Jennifer, if you finish early, would you like to plan and lead the discussion tomorrow on the novel we're reading?"

Challenge with Choice Strategy #4: Self-Individualized Scaffolding

Scaffolding is a relatively recent (or at least, "rediscovered") word for a strategy that good teachers have been doing intuitively all along. Scaffolding is simply your effort to provide more structure, more modeling, and more cues in the earlier stages of any learning experience. As your students become more proficient in using the skills or content unassisted, the scaffolding is removed. Scaffolding helps students to gradually become more independent, or autonomous, as learners.

Dialogue with your students so they have some choice about how much structure and modeling they need for a task. For example, kindergartners will want to be able to do things without your help. Say, "Tell me when you want a clue if you get stuck." This way, you'll be producing more self-reliant learners.

Students will become less dependent on you, and you'll be able to expect—and get—more quality work out of them. They will take more pride in their accomplishments because they did it themselves! They will grow in their level of responsibility. Your classroom will become more and more like a team, as members push themselves to perform at their highest level of capability.

Challenge with Choice Strategy #5: Just-Right Reading

This strategy follows naturally from self-individualized scaffolding in the previous strategy. Your goal is to foster in children the ability to select reading material that is at the "just-right" level. This is enormously important! There is no possible way you want to be spending your time with 2nd graders individually hand-picking a book for each and every child day after day. And clearly, given the singularly crucial influence of reading ability on a child's success in school, you want each child to enjoy reading. And that means they must be trained in how to select reading material that will be enjoyable to them—not too easy and not too difficult. Initially, you will probably engage in both whole-group as well as one-to-one instruction with the children. Eventually, the majority of the children will be proficient at selecting their own reading material. This frees up your time, makes you and the children more successful, and is a joyful outcome to experience.

Challenge with Choice Strategy #6: Project-Based Learning

This is perhaps the epitome of execution of challenge with choice. On nearly every occasion that I have had students engage in longer-term, complex, engaging projects, I have seen my highly capable students go far beyond what I required. And at the same time with the same project, I have seen my less capable learners feel safe, enjoy themselves, make greater efforts to do their best, and generally learn far more than with briefer lessons. Individual students demonstrated talents that I did not even know they had. By the time children are in 3rd or 4th grade, project-based learning can certainly be a strategy within your win-win instructional repertoire.

■ THE "PLEASANT AND PATIENT" STRATEGY

It is easy to forget the importance of being patient. Each day, continue to nurture your rapport with underachieving and at-risk children. And be patient. And nurture the rapport day after day after day without losing your patience or taking it personally. And each step of the way, invite the student to choose learning and engagement instead of apathy, fear, or other counterproductive attitudes.

Over time, a great number of your difficult students will choose to improve in the presence of a trusting, caring, patient, pleasant, enthusiastic teacher. It takes the relationship, and the relationship takes time. How much time? This you know in hindsight only. And as the relationship happens, you want to raise your expectations without jeopardizing the rapport. This is the essence of good coaching and good counseling.

The patience is crucial. Students' brains have accumulated memory upon memory in their mental photo albums. Your job is to flood their lives (to the extent possible within a school day) with positive pictures. Eventually . . . slowly . . . days or weeks or months or even years later . . . the positive pictures may just possibly overwhelm the negative ones. And at that point, success will be visible.

However, it is possible that you will *never* see the results of your nurturing and patience. You are only human. They are only human. There's only so much you can do.

In the best of cases, you help the student to erase some of their negative pictures. However, some of these pictures—such as those that result from abuse, neglect, or a serious auto accident—will not go away. The memory endures, but the passage of time causes the memory to recede and to lose importance, *especially* if more recent memories are positive. You can only hope that the positive memories you are able to facilitate with your students will *be enough*, and *be soon enough*, to make a difference in your classroom this year.

An Example . . .

Robert, an at-risk minority student, came to my high-school science class in September unprepared, apathetic, unsmiling, ready for battle. I was nice to him. He handed in no work that month. I was nice to him. In October, he still did nothing. I could have been sterner with him, though the likely result is that he would have dropped out of my class, and out of school, that much sooner. By November, he smiled and actually talked to me. He still did no work. By December, we truly enjoyed each other, and *finally he decided on his own that he wanted to learn!* It took more than three months for me to build enough trust with Robert that the positive pictures were now displacing the negative ones. It is doubtful that a teacher who rushes the process will succeed any better or any faster.

The more a student respects you, and the more rapport you have, the more you can raise your expectations without fear of antagonizing or alienating the student. What you want is to push the student as far as you can without jeopardizing the relationship. When they like you, you can push them further.

It took months or years for students to accumulate their album of mental pictures that drives their emotions and perceptions. This album takes time to modify.

■ Your Positive Self-Talk: "The Glass Is Half Full, Not Half Empty"

Reflect upon, and take pride in, the students you *are* reaching, rather than dwelling on the students you are *not* reaching. It may be counterintuitive, but when you mentally celebrate the students you are reaching, you not only reach these better, but are also likely to reach your difficult students at the same time. The reasoning is as follows: By adopting more positive self-talk, your attitude, optimism, and body language communicate to all students that you are confident, enthusiastic, and good-natured and that you enjoy your students. Your positive self-talk builds relationships. These positive thoughts energize you.

Read this next sentence two or three times and memorize it! "When my thoughts are consumed by the students I am *not* reaching, I can easily become less effective with all of my students—even the ones I *had* been reaching!"

Chapter 19
Being Inspired and Inspiring

My own beliefs are stated or implied throughout this book. These are my biases, my values. They have influenced much of this book's direction and content. They drive and energize my teaching, and as a consequence, these beliefs have inspired so many hundreds of teachers who have participated in my workshops. Being *inspired* leads to being *inspiring*. And that leads to being effective.

■ INSPIRED TEACHING: WHAT IS IT, AND WHAT DIFFERENCE DOES IT MAKE?

In my workshops, I often ask teachers to brainstorm for a couple of minutes the feelings, experiences, and results they associate with the concept of "being inspired." In no time at all, we have a substantial list of items such as having more energy, being more productive, having more patience with kids, enjoying myself, losing track of time, getting excited about life, and feeling confident. We then construct a simple concept map to show just how many powerful effects result from this state of energy or inspiration. Not surprisingly, these results spin off into other positive results. And we have the rather wonderful state whereby the results themselves feed right back into the upward spiral, giving us yet more energy and inspiration. All of which illustrates the concept of multiplier effects—the benefits multiply over time, and extend into our wellness outside of school, and into our relationships with friends and family as well.

So here is the answer to the question "What difference does it make if I am inspired when I'm teaching?" When you feel inspired, your enthusiasm, tone of voice, and body language are all more welcoming and effective with your students. Just the fact of being inspired will in all likelihood reduce classroom management problems and give you more time to teach. Kids will listen more attentively, and that results in more learning. Kids will be more emotionally engaged, and that results in both more learning *and* more retention. You will smile and laugh more, which reduces your stress level, and leaves you with more energy at the end of the day. You will be more productive, think more clearly, and be more creative—all of which foster your capacity to design better lessons and to more fully tap all of your teaching wisdom. We do our best teaching when we feel in control, when we exercise choice, and when we have ownership.

Thus, investing in your own inspiration is one of the single most powerful things you can do for your teaching and for your life.

Additionally, you persevere more when you *really* value something. At the least, the students realize that you will be relentless and consistent in your beliefs and actions. And students want and need strong leaders who are relentless. The result is that your message gets through more strongly, and your students buy in more quickly.

On the other hand, when you care less about something, there is less energy in your commitment. You tend to lower your expectations and give in more readily. This jeopardizes students' trust in your consistency, resilience, and persistence. As soon as you give up, students give up. Or they exploit your moments of weakness.

■ Your Inspiration Applied

I suggest that one of your goals might be to find ways to tap into your inspiration and energy while *simultaneously* teaching the standards or curriculum that you are required to teach.

Find and Teach That Which Energizes You

Sometimes, we care deeply about something but forget to tell the kids. We just assume they know . . . that we care, or that we love learning, or that we believe everyone deserves respect. Go a step further and articulate to your students your strongly held beliefs about teaching, about learning, and about your subject areas. These efforts only take a few moments, but they can make a huge difference.

Use Your Own Stories

Your life's stories convey a message that aligns with your body language and communicate emotion, integrity, and ownership. It is partly through your stories that you can become such a powerful role model, even a hero, to these children.

Reinforce It, Model It, Reteach It—Week after Week

On another day, or another week, revisit briefly that same story or example. Or design a lesson to teach or model it. For example, if you believe strongly that your students will be successful, choose children's literature that reinforces this theme. Let your passionate beliefs benefit from repetition in various contexts. You can readily integrate these beliefs into the curriculum—if your students have to practice grammar and writing, let them write about a success they have had.

Find examples of it. Have students find examples of it. When a student perseveres and is successful, ask, "How does that feel?" Or say, "Wow, that makes me so incredibly happy, because it is one of the things I care so much about. Thank you."

Chapter 20
Advanced Orchestration

■ Planning Lessons with Your Repertoire: An Example

It is 4:00 PM Tuesday afternoon. It was a long day. I had hoped to have 60 minutes to prepare tomorrow's social studies lesson, related to the American Revolution, but it looks like I will have only 15 minutes. Let's throw in a couple more constraints: (1) I want something that will motivate them enough that I will not have to threaten them with collecting and grading it; (2) I don't want to have to create or photocopy a worksheet; and (3) I want my at-risk learners to be engaged as well. What to do?

I take a look at my *reminder list*. I want to start with something that is low-stress and gets kids involved: "You have 60 seconds working in groups to *list* every word, person, or event that comes to mind when you think of the American Revolution." Now that students have tapped into at least some of their prior knowledge, perhaps you can ask them, "Pick out your favorite five, and share with us why you picked those." This is the *rate, evaluate, judge* tool. This will lead into a *scenario*: "You take a time machine back to the time of George Washington. Your job is to hand George a thank-you letter from the twenty-first century. He did, after all, help us to win the Revolution. Think of just a few things you want to thank George for. Plus, because George will be very pleasantly surprised to hear from you, and very surprised that this country still exists, do let him know a few other things you think would make for entertaining reading. Oh, and for those of you who were impressed with the penmanship in the Declaration of Independence, I brought in some calligraphy pens and highlighters (*using color*) for visual impact—these are optional." And now for an *audience beyond the teacher:* "I am looking forward to how creative these will be." At this point, I tell students we can compile their letters into a book, or invite the principal in to hear us read them, or send them to our local paper for publication just before President's Day. Meanwhile, if I have the time or inclination, I can certainly brainstorm with the kids what a good thank-you letter would look like—this is the *criteria-setting* tool—and maybe go so far as having students *self-assess* their letters according to our criteria.

The above lesson is not perfect; lessons never are. Rather, it is a tolerably decent use of a mere 10 or 15 minutes to create a lesson that will engage students in thinking and learning. (Actually, I timed myself, and the entire lesson plan took me 8 minutes to construct.) Done—no photocopying, no materials, and there is enough flexibility built into it that I can easily modify the lesson for individual students. Sure, I can make this lesson better. With time, most lessons will be made better. The point is this: time is our scarcest resource, and if we have ready access to a versatile, win-win repertoire, we are at least better off than we would have been. (Hey, and another benefit: all that photocopying that you and your colleagues are now able to skip saves money and trees.)

■ Running the Parts on Autopilot

Your goal is to execute the parts of the lesson on autopilot. You then free yourself to actively orchestrate the whole.

Know your tools so well that you can use them when you're half-asleep. Focus your energies on the choice of tool and its application to your particular situation: Which tool fits this objective? How do I need to change the tool to make the learning easier, or more challenging? Which tools flow nicely together and reach the full diversity of my students?

Take small steps. Gradual changes in your instruction or expectations may help you feel safer—and saner—than abrupt and drastic changes. Remember . . . if you burn out, it doesn't do anyone any good.

■ Reverse Planning

Usually in your planning, you probably think first about the lesson or unit objective, and then generate the lesson activity. Try the reverse. Start with something that would engage kids, and say to yourself, "There's got to be something useful I can teach with this." Given that many of you have perhaps 170 days with your students and a long list of learning objectives, it is very likely that somewhere in the school year, the engaging activity would adapt itself perfectly to a meaningful objective. Especially when you consider that fostering a positive classroom environment is one of your priorities.

This reverse thinking helps you to use some of your best stuff for engaging your students. All you need to do is find ways for this best stuff to teach the curriculum.

For example, I have a handheld Global Positioning System (GPS) unit. Amazingly—if you've never seen one of these—this little gadget finds satellites orbiting the earth, and then does some computer calculations to pinpoint your latitude and longitude with an accuracy of 15 feet. Very impressive! Reverse planning idea: "OK, this would engage kids—at least the ones who love gadgets. I can get some of the kids to actually read the instruction booklet to figure out how it works (*reading*). I can work with them on learning latitude and longitude, and seeing if the GPS unit is accurate by checking a map for our location (*map work*). I can just play around with it during recess with a couple of my underachievers (*strategic relevance*)."

■ Expanding Your Repertoire

Two key points: First, your success with any tool or technique depends so much on the relationship you have with your students, the way you manage your classroom, and your artful orchestration of your teaching objectives. All of this depends greatly on your own physical and emotional wellness. Remember to take care of yourself. Have a life outside of school. Remember to laugh.

Second, apply your own wisdom, common sense, and energy. Be comforted to know there are no "Tools Police." These tools, and the labels used, are merely prompts for your own thinking. Experiment. Adapt them however you wish. Your goal is to foster results that exceed the effort invested.

Inventory Your Repertoire

Reflect on the following three elements as you inventory your repertoire. You'll then be able to focus your efforts where they will provide the most benefits.

Quantity: Do you have a large number of instructional tools? Do you have alternative ways to structure your classroom cooperatively? Or to foster student thinking? Or to practice previously learned concepts? Or do you find yourself repeating a relatively small number of teaching methods and activities?

Variety: Do you readily teach your content using a wide spectrum of experiences, for example, creative or logical, visual or hands-on, musical or kinesthetic, playfully spontaneous or seriously organized?

It takes variety to reach all parts of the brain, and to reach all learners' talents and interests. It takes variety to maintain your students' alert mental state. Also search your repertoire for weaker areas or gaps. For example, perhaps you have a strong repertoire in math but are weaker in reading. Or you have a repertoire for building a positive classroom climate but less of a repertoire for fostering student self-reliance and independent thinking.

Flexibility: Do your tools put you in charge of your lessons, or are they fixed recipes that are difficult to adapt to different learners? Can you quickly and spontaneously adapt these tools to teachable moments? Remember, time is scarce. You want tools that take less of your effort or time.

■ Exploiting Your Successes (Especially the Unexpected Ones)

Of the many lessons, organizational schemes, and teaching styles that we try during a year, some will succeed far more than others. Analyze these happy and sometimes unexpected successes. For example, if your students were spectacularly engaged with a dinosaur unit, do not automatically assume that the key factor was dinosaurs (though that might be true). Perhaps it was the fact that you were more animated during that unit. Or that there was more hands-on learning. Or the approach was more playful. Or connected more with students' prior knowledge.

Once you come up with a working hypothesis as to what the key factors were, you can now exploit that knowledge by incorporating those attributes into other lessons. For example, if it really was dinosaurs that motivated the students, then by all means, dinosaurs should be incorporated into math word problems, into writing, and into reading. This simple analysis will pay you back *big*—it means that you can quickly improve student learning by tapping what you are already doing well. This takes far less time than searching outside yourself for lessons and teaching methods that might work. Furthermore, you get to stay within your comfort zone, which reduces your stress level and lets you be more relaxed and authentic with students.

Always tap first what is within your brain and within your repertoire. (It's like grocery shopping: check the fridge before you go! In this case, first check your own mind before you go searching other peoples' minds.)

Sanity-saving recommendation: Reflect upon and exploit whichever unexpected successes you experience. When something works, find out what it was that worked and replicate that component within other lessons and other curriculum areas. By this means, you may come to fully appreciate (as I did) the remarkable power of such strategies as one-to-one time, strategic irrelevance, challenge with choice, and others.

From Your Repertoire to Extraordinary Learning

When students are excited to engage, learning and long-term retention are fostered. And what nurtures this motivation? Opportunities to explore interests in depth. To have choices with meaningful challenges. To create authentic projects. To have fun. And to do all of this within a supportive community of learners. The result can be some extraordinary learning.

All of which takes your flexibility, because each day's lessons now are more attuned to the present teachable moments and are less predictable or controllable. This leads right back to why you want to have ready access to a rich repertoire of simple, enjoyable techniques.

So refer often to these tools. Keep a reminder list and put sticky notes in your plan book to ensure you frequently incorporate many of these quick, yet powerful, tools.

Reminders

This is an appropriate place to step back and review what we have explored so far.

Your challenge: Time is scarce. You have a wide variety of students. How do you invest your time to get the greatest return, and to maintain your long-term enthusiasm for teaching?

The answer: Invest your time so that smaller and more pleasurable efforts now produce enduring, ever multiplying benefits that perpetuate themselves. These multiplier effects emerge from the following:

Advanced Orchestration 153

> Your own physical and emotional wellness, combined with an optimistic outlook, are pivotal to your effectiveness. The very direction your wellness and attitude are spiraling tends to perpetuate itself. Invest in yourself, and not just in your students—this is win-win teaching.
>
> Get clear on who you are, what you believe, and your teaching methods.
>
> Create efficient, predictable classroom routines. Create a classroom culture where you and your students jointly feel ownership of these routines. Otherwise, you'll end up doing too much of the work.
>
> Build a rich, diverse, enjoyable, and *simple* repertoire. And use a reminder list so you do, in fact, exploit your repertoire.
>
> Add variety, novelty, and play to your routines.
>
> Nurture a high-trust classroom environment.
>
> Invest in one-to-one time with students.
>
> Facilitate a classroom environment increasingly organized to provide challenge with choice, and nurture students' ability and willingness to "self-individualize" their learning.
>
> Whenever possible, make the learning relevant and authentic.

In conclusion, remember that for as long as you care deeply about children, teaching will rarely become easy, but it can be easier than it is.

Experiment. Enjoy.

Bibliography

Borba, Michele. 1988. *Esteem Builders: A K–8 Self-Esteem Curriculum for Improving Student Achievement Behavior and School Climate.* Austin, TX: Jalmar Press.

Covey, Stephen R. 2004. *The 7 Habits of Highly Effective People.* Northampton, MA: Free Press.

de Bono, Edward. 1985. *De Bono's Thinking Course.* New York: Facts on File Publications.

Dennison, Paul E., and Gail Dennison. 1989. *Brain Gym: Teacher's Edition.* Ventura, CA: Edu-Kinesthetics.

Fay, Jim, and David Funk. 1998. *Teaching with Love and Logic: Taking Control of the Classroom.* Golden, CO: Love & Logic Press.

Glasser, William. 1998. *The Quality School.* New York: Perennial.

Hunter, Madeline. 1982. *Mastery Teaching.* Englewood, CO: TIP Publications.

Jensen, Eric. 1988. *Super-Teaching: Master Strategies for Building Student Success.* Del Mar, CA: Turning Point.

———. 2005. *Teaching with the Brain in Mind.* Alexandria, VA: Association for Supervision & Curriculum.

Kagan, Spencer. 1997. *Cooperative Learning.* San Clemente, CA: Kagan Publishing.

Kessler, Rachael. 2000. *The Soul of Education: Helping Students Find Connection, Compassion, and Character at School.* San Clemente, CA: Association for Supervision & Curriculum.

Koch, Kenneth. 1999. *Wishes, Lies, and Dreams: Teaching Children to Write Poetry.* New York: HarperCollins.

Marzano, Robert J., et al., eds. 2001. *A Handbook for Classroom Instruction That Works.* San Clemente, CA: Association for Supervision & Curriculum.

———. 2003. *Classroom Management That Works: Research-based Strategies for Every Teacher.* San Clemente, CA: Association for Supervision & Curriculum.

National Research Council. 2000. *How People Learn: Brain, Mind, Experience, and School.* Exp. ed. Washington, DC: National Academies Press.

Nelsen, Jane. 2000. *Positive Discipline in the Classroom: Developing Mutual Respect, Cooperation, and Responsibility in Your Classroom.* Rev. 3rd ed. New York: Three Rivers Press.

Routman, Regie. 2003. *Reading Essentials.* Portsmouth, NH: Heinemann.

Steinberg, Adria, and Kathleen Cushman. 1999. *Schooling for the Real World: A Guide to Providing Enriching Classroom Learning Experiences.* San Francisco, CA: Jossey-Bass.

Stock, Gregory. 2004. *The Kids' Book of Questions: Revised for the New Century.* New York: Workman Publishing Company.

Van Matre, Steve. 1972. *Acclimatization: A Personal and Reflective Approach to a Natural Relationship.* Martinsville, IN: American Camping Association.

Weinstein, Matt, and Joel Goodman. 1980. *Playfair: Everybody's Guide to Non-competitive Play.* New York: Impact Publishing.

Wiggins, Grant, and Jay McTighe. 2000. *Understanding by Design.* San Luis Obispo, CA: Prentice-Hall.

Wong, Harry K., and Rosemary T. Wong. 2004. *The First Days of School: How to Be an Effective Teacher.* Mountain View, CA: Harry K. Wong Publications.

Index

Abstract-concept art, 109
Acronyms, 55
Acrostic name displays, 31
Advertisements, 122
Aerobic exercise, 127
Affirmations, 32
Alliteration, 57
Analogy, 60
Anecdotes, 16
Answer-to-question review, 125
Appropriate choice, 142
Art, 108
Assignment menus, 118
Audiences, 37, 122
Authentic audiences, 37, 122
Authentic creativity with products and technologies, 121
Authentic dilemmas, 35
Authentic error searches, 97
Authentic examples, 36
Authentic investigations, 120
Authentic leadership roles, 116
Authentic learning, 36
Authentic letter-writing, 38
Authentic problem-solving, 119
Authentic reasons, 36
Authentic skills dramatization, 111
Authentic visitors, 122
Authentic voice, 35
Autobiographical drawings, 109
Autopilot, 150

Awards, 75

Back drawings, 54
Background music, 113
Balloons and static electricity, 51
Before/after sequence game, 102
Best-case/worst-case scenarios, 20
Biographical drawings, 109
Bird nests, 49
Brainstorming, 92
Breathing, 126
Bridge design, 49
Business interviews, 39

Calligraphy, 25
Celebrations, 76
Challenge and choice, 141
Changes game, 78
Charades, 55
Circle role-play game, 88
Classifying tasks, 98
Class names, 76
Classroom meetings, 26
Coalition of Essential Schools, 22
Coat hanger chime, 50
Collaboration, 70
Collaborative displays, 72
Collaborative note-taking, 124
Collaborative poems, 63
Collaborative storytelling, 59
Collaborative writing, 62

Color-coding, 25
Comments box, 33
Communication precision tools, 53, 54
Compare/contrast, 105
Compliments, 31
Concept drawings, 109
Concept mapping, 45
Connecting eyes circle, 87
Consequence chain, 46
Consequence map, 46
Constraint tasks, 4
Cooperative role definition, 71
Cotton balls in water, 49
Counting-circles, 100
Creative brainstorms, 93
Creative design, 49
Creative imagery, 23
Creative labels, 56
Creative math completions, 96
Creative mode, 45
Creative thinking modes, 45
Criteria-setting, 67
Cross-age collaboration, 71
Current issues problem-solving, 120
Cut and paste, 114

Data collection, 52
de Bono, Edward, 93
Decision-making, 116
Decision-making across curriculum, 117
Dedications ceremonies, 75
Deductive logic, 106
Design technology, 48
Desk organization blueprints, 110
Dialogue, 26, 125
Discoveries, 104
Discrepant events, 49
Divergent tasks, 40
Do-as-I-do games, 81
Doodle art, 108
Dramatization, 111
Drum roll, 112
Duration versus impact, 14
Dust-buddies, 3

Egg drop, 49
Eleven, 86
Endorphin replays, 135
Errors search, 97
Essential questions, 22

Esteem-building, 31
Estimate, 41
Estimating games, 42
Event drawings, 109
Experimental design, 52
Exploiting your successes, 151

Family interviews, 39
Fantasy, 83
Fantasy guests, 83
Fay, Jim, 132
Feedback, 32
Feedback sheets, 34
Fictional report cards, 57
Find your own, 78
Finger math game, 86
Fizz-buzz, 101
Fluid organization, 6
Focus shifts, 46
Focus words, 31
Freewrites, 64
Frozen role-play, 112
Funk, David, 132

Games design, 48
Goal-setting, 116
Good luck, 14
Graphic organizers, 45
Gravity grab, 85
Grouping tasks, 98
Guest speakers, 39

Hand-squeeze circle, 86
Hidden-pass circle, 87
Highlighting, 25
How-to writing, 54
Human electricity, 86
Humor, 22, 83
Hypothesize/estimate/predict, 41

"I am" statements, 32
Idea time, 30
Imagery, 23
Images circle, 73
Improvements brainstorm, 92
Index to your brain, 132
Information literacy, 122
Inquiry, 52
Inspired teaching, 147
Interest surveys, 32

Index

Interviews, 38
Invisible glue, 83
Invitational choices, 144
I wonder, 29

Johnny Oops, 81
Journal-writing menu, 64
Just noticing, 12
Just-right reading, 145
Just watching, 34

Keepers, 29
Kessler, Rachael, 27
Key-word note-taking, 124

Learner-centered dialogue, 26
Lesson planning, 149
Letter exchanges, 38
Letters to yourself, 38
Line-by-line poems, 62
Line-up games, 74
Listen-think-do, 94
Listing, 4, 90
Logic, 106
Lottery tickets, 75

Macadamia nut, 50
Magic, 82
Magic bottle, 83
Map drawing, 110
Marzano, Robert, 1
Math art, 108
Measuring games, 42
Meet your neighbor, 88
Memory games, 78
Mental maps, 137
Me riddles, 32
Message chains, 54
Metaphor, 60
Metaphorical art, 109
Micro-notes, 124
Mini-rituals, 76
Mnemonics, 56
Mottoes, 76
Music, 113
Mysterious footprints, 83
Mystery person, 32

Name circle, 102
Neat stuff box, 7

Nelson, Jane, 27
Nim, 100
Note-taking, 123
Novel manipulatives, 114

Observation centers, 24
Observation games, 77
Observation memory game, 78
One-to-one time, 11
Open-ended questions, 27
Orchestration, 129, 149
Outrageous story math, 59
Outrageous truths list, 58

Packaging, 22
Paired sharing, 71
Paired sharing journals, 64
Pairing games, 103
Pairs of pairs, 72
Paper airplane contest, 48
Partner introductions, 30
Parts of the system, 50
Patient-and-pleasant strategy, 145
Peer-to-peer support, 70
Personal celebrations, 136
Personalizing assignments, 15
Personalizing classroom, 15
Personalizing discussion, 15
Physically active games, 85
Picnic, 80
Picture charades, 55
Picture note-taking, 123
Plan B, 118
Plant germination/growth, 51
Play, 139
Playful repetitions, 57
Poetry, 62
Positive, interesting, negative (PIN), 93
Positive self-talk, 146
Posted answers, 143
Practical imagery, 23
Predict, 41
Problem-solving, 119
Process dramatization, 112
Process sharing, 43
Project-based learning, 145
Project packets, 119
Props, 21

Question/answer plays, 56

Question circle, 73
Question of the day, 29
Questions list, 29
Quotations, 59

Randomization technique, 106
Rate, evaluate, judge, 27, 65
Readers theater, 85
Real voice, 35
Recollection tasks, 28
Relaxation, 126
Relaxation imagery, 23
Reminder list, 132
Repertoire, 1, 5, 44
Repertoire inventory, 151
Repertoire lesson-planning, 149
Response repertoires, 44
Responsibility questions, 125
Reverse planning, 150
Role-playing, 111
Role-plays for responsibility and self-discipline, 125
Round robin, 72

Safari, 80
Scaffolding, 144
Scale drawings, 110
Scavenger hunt, 4, 96
Scenario challenges, 20
Scenario headlines, 21
Scenario predictions, 21
Scenarios, 17
Scientific thinking, 50, 52
Search tasks, 4, 12, 96
Secret code games, 81
Secret pals, 75
Secrets, 15
Secret sorting, 79
Seed poems, 63
Self-assessments, 28, 68
Self-awareness, 125
Self-discipline questions, 125
Self-efficacy, 115
Self-esteem, 115
Self-individualization, 142
Self-individualized scaffolding, 144
Self-questionnaire, 30
Self-reliance, 125
Self-sorting, 77
Self-talk, 146

Sensory box, 78
Sensory experiences, 113
Sensory novelty, 114
Sentence chains, 54
Sentence stems, 95
Sequence circle, 102
Sequencing tasks, 98, 99
Serial response games, 100
Shared feelings, 30
Sharing circles, 72
Sharing circle with movement, 73
Sharing pairs, 72
Signal groupings, 74
Simultaneous modalities circle, 101
Social studies systems design, 51
Spatial conceptualization drawings, 110
Spelling circle, 100
Staff development, x
Standing ovation, 76
Standoff, 85
Static electricity, 51
Stems, 94
Sticky-note feedback, 33
Sticky notes, 132
Story predictions, 95
Storytelling grid, 59
Storytelling, playful, 57
Strategic irrelevance, 12
Stress reduction, 126
Stretching and movement, 127
Student-centered learning, 36
Student-generated questions, 37
Student-initiated service, 126
Student-initiated statements, 29
Student self-assessment, 28, 68
Students teaching teachers, 14
Success imagery, 24
Suggestions box, 33
Surveys and data collection, 52
Systems, 50
Systems design, 47

Tactile writing, 113
Task lists, 103
Task rotations, 84
Task series technique, 94
Teacher-friendly choices, 143
Teacher voice, 35
Teaching with Love and Logic (Fay and Funk), 132

Tense and relax, 127
Thinking aloud, 43
Three-minute actions, 136
Three truths, 58
Tillie Williams, 80
Time constraints, 4
Time lines, 104
Time management logs, 119
Time travel scenarios, 19
To-do lists, 103
Trial runs, 131
Trust-building play, 87
Turn to a neighbor, 71

Unanswered questions, 29
Underachievers, 141
Upward spirals, 134

Values tasks, 27, 66
VIP letters, 38
Visual enhancement, 24
Visualization, 23
Vocabulary of personal attributes, 126
Volunteers, choosing student, 80
Voting, 67

Wait time, 44
Water drops on a penny, 50
What-if scenarios, 18
What's my rule games, 79
Whose story is it, 58
Word associations brainstorm, 92
Word banks, 56
Word collections, 56

Yawning, 127

About the Author

KENNETH L. WILSON is an Education and Training Consultant from Seattle, Washington and a senior faculty member of The Heritage Institute, Clinton, Washington.

www.ingramcontent.com/pod-product-compliance
Lightning Source LLC
Chambersburg PA
CBHW081203240426
43669CB00039B/2792